STONE SOUP

Morsels of an Unsettled Life

By Anita Lobel

Also by the Author

No Pretty Pictures: A Child of War

(1998, National Book Award Nominee)

Copyright 2020, 2021, 2022 by Anita Lobel

Presto Publishing, New York, New York

Dedication

To the memory of my great and true love, Billy Giles, forever and ever. And, to my dear friend and counselor, Doug Whiteman, with love and thanks for wise guidance and great humor.

[4]

TABLE OF CONTENTS

Prologue

Arriving

Later

Later Still

Real Estate

"Tomorrow and Tomorrow..."

Cassandra

Wine Bar

Attack

Twists and Turnarounds

Encounter

Palladio

Medford and Matisse

Shards

Halloween Parade

"Yet It Will Come"

Once Upon a Time... and Later

Paris Interlude: Waiting

Epilogue: A Christmas Up North

"The moment you put pen to paper, autobiographical writing becomes autofiction."

Anita Lobel

PROLOGUE

There is always a beginning. There has to be. This one was mine.

I was five years old when I watched Nazis march into Kraków. Very soon three of them came to bang on our apartment door. They pushed their way in and took many things. First Tata left. Then Mama went away, too. Niania and I left the city and went to live far away in the country. When Niania found out that Nazis were coming to look for Jews hiding in our village, we left. We fled to another village. I was seven years old. We heard nothing from Mama or Tata. We didn't know where they were. When I was nine years old Niania and I went back to the city. We stayed with nuns in a convent. On Christmas morning we were at Mass in the chapel. Nazis burst in. The singing stopped. I was hauled outside. They pushed me toward the convent wall. I could feel the icy brick against my nose and forehead. One Nazi stuck his gun behind my right ear. He didn't shoot. He turned me around and shoved me into a canvas covered truck. Niania was kicked away and left behind because she was not a Jew. The truck drove to a big prison. Before the Nazis came, dangerous criminals had been locked in there. Now it was filled with captured Jews. Then, one night the Nazis opened the cells and we were marched through empty, dark Kraków streets. We came to a deserted train station and were forced to climb into the cars of a waiting train without windows. I was packed with many people standing, pushing against me. After a long ride the train came to a stop. Not everyone got off. Some had died standing up during the trip. We marched some more through freezing snow and winds until we got to a place with rows of gray buildings that were surrounded with tall fences of barbed wire. Blinding lights were shining on us. The Nazis lined us up and yelled and counted everyone. They divided us into groups and pushed us into the buildings called barracks.

They cut off my braids and shaved my head. For a long, long time I lay on a cot of straw covered in dirty burlap. I shivered and leaked dysentery. I never stopped itching and scratching because of the lice in the seams of my raggedy clothes. I tried to remember nice times from when I was very little. I dreamed of white rolls with butter. I dreamed that Niania was coming for me.

Niania never came. But, one day, good soldiers did. They sliced the barbed wire and took the guns from the Nazis and drove them away in canvas covered trucks. Other good people came and gave us fresh clothes and food. Then, we rode in their white buses through thick, dark forests. There was gunfire all around and bombs falling from above. In the morning, we arrived safely at a shore. We were put on a boat to cross to another land.

I didn't understand what people were saying to me. But I understood that I was sick. I had a sickness in my lungs. I lay in bed for many months. This bed had white sheets and soft pillows and warm blankets. I always had good food and clean clothes. I went for

walks in green fields and woods with other patients. I got better. Mama and Papa were found. They came to get me. We went to live in a beautiful city called Stockholm. I liked being a girl with parents.
When I was thirteen and fourteen and fifteen I had teachers, who taught me how to look and listen and search below that which was on the surface and obvious in the world. I had friends who taught me how to laugh and swim and dance, making me feel good and worthy of their company. I sang in a church choir and loved celebrating Swedish Christmas with my friends. When I was almost seventeen my parents told me we were leaving Stockholm, Sweden to go to America.

At Centralen, the main railroad station in Stockholm, friends and teachers came to cry and embrace me and to give me books and mementos. We promised, promised, promised...,! This was not good-bye forever, no!.. A time for return would come, yes, yes, yes,..!

But we couldn't stop the wheels of the train on the rails from beginning to roll, taking me away. In the noise of their gathering speed I heard, forrr-ever, forrr-ever, forrr-ever,......clack, clack, clack,-no going back,..clack..... I left behind everything I had come to love. It was then I no longer wanted to be the child of my parents.

ARRIVING

New York City

1.

During the fourteen days of crossing, the old "Gripsholm" passenger vessel withstood winter storms and heaving seas. Sailing into New York harbor past the Statue of Liberty, escorted by tugboats, we docked at the 57th street berth of The Swedish America Line. We disembarked to the sounds and noise of waterway traffic behind us, and the cacophony of the City before us. From across a barrier my parents spotted the relatives. Those distant cousins they had never met, who were to become a replacement for all the loved people forever taken from them by murderers.

Because of a file of health certificates one of those relations had neglected to bring to the right immigration authorities in time for our arrival, we were taken from the busy giant arrival area to a ferry boat that deposited us and our pile of luggage in a big building in a place named Ellis Island. Here we waited with others who also were not yet granted permission to enter the land of promise. It took more than a week for the mix-up to be set to right. At last we were allowed to border the ferry and enter the island of Manhattan.

Until permanent lodging could be found, we were warehoused in a crowded temporary shelter run by a Jewish organization in a converted old library on Astor Place. In its scaffolded, improvised partitions forming semiprivate cubicles, I was once again sleeping on an institutional bunk bed. Not made of straw and covered with filthy burlap rags. No. It had a mattress and a pillow and sheets and blankets. The building was not surrounded by barbed wire. It was not patrolled by Nazi guards. The doors were not locked. But once again I was in a holding tank in exile.

Sometime later, with the help of the same Jewish organization, an apartment was found in a tenement building in Brooklyn. My dreary little room had a floor covered with speckled linoleum and a window facing a gloomy shaft. I was stunned and angry and diminished and without any expectation of a new rescue.

The family, with whom my parents had so longed to be reunited, consisted of a married first cousin of my father's. She and her husband had escaped from Berlin with not much more than the clothes on their backs right before the Anschluss. They never ceased to be suspicious of everyone and lived in unspecified fear of everything still. The man worked as a cutter in the clothing industry. The wife did not have a job. On my mother's side, there was a quartet of middle aged, unmarried second cousins: two plain sisters and two of their older, charmless brothers whose parents had come to America after the First World War. All these people lived in apartments not far from each other in the Eastern Parkway section of Brooklyn.

One sister was a grade school teacher, one a bank teller. The brothers were clerks in small business companies. Very little help with settling in or the loan of even a small amount of money my parents had counted on, was forthcoming from any of these people. They didn't and, I knew, never would mean anything to me. To my parents they were "Family!" "Family!"

I had completed almost four years of Swedish high school. I had attended evening classes at a Stockholm art academy. I carried with me a file of my grades and my student artwork in a cardboard portfolio tied with strings. Before applying to an art college I had to go back to high school and find my way to an American diploma.

One evening at the apartment of the married cousins, a young neighbor, a veteran, who had marched with the liberating Yanks into Paris in August 1944, curious to meet the newly arrived, dropped in. He was an engineering student. His university studies were paid for with money from something called the GI bill. I mentioned that I very much hoped to go to an art school.

He suggested that I apply to an all girl public high school in Manhattan, known for its art classes. The former GI had a friend whose sister had been a student there. Upon graduation, she was accepted at an art college. He volunteered to make a phone call to arrange an interview for me. For the first time since we had set foot in New York, I felt as though, into the apartment of the scared of everything cousins, a practical, rescuing angel had descended, with a glimmer of hope to wrap myself in.

A few days later I rode the New Lots train from far-out Brooklyn to the Union Square stop in Manhattan. I hated the noisy, rattling, old underground trains. The stations smelled of electricity and dampness trapped in old cellars. The crowds of riders reeked of underarm deodorant, hair gel and chewing gum. I hung on to straps, flinching from the touch of clammy hands and knitted gloves. Riders peered at newspapers folded in half, held closely to the body by those who had managed to squeeze into seats. To me the word "subway" was peculiar. Why wasn't it called the "underground?" Exit signs confused me. I couldn't tell if "Exit" meant to point to nearby stairs to the street or to passages to other connecting trains. Mostly, I was too self conscious about asking directions.

All my Stockholm transportation had been above ground with air and sunlight streaming through windows of clanging trolley cars and buses. Blasting and excavations for the new below ground rail system, the "tunnelbanan," had only just begun. It would be shiny and clean and smooth and quiet on the rails. Would I ever go back to ride with my friends in one of the new trains? Would I ever even see my friends again?
Now I was packed into an old, screechy "subway" riding in the direction of "Uptown" to appear before an unfamiliar someone who might allow me to become a student in an American school. In my mind I imagined

questions I ought to be prepared for. I rehearsed words and phrases in English, hoping I might present a smart enough new arrival, worthy and eager of acceptance into a new life in New York City.

After the more than one hour ride, I stepped out of the train onto a platform, found the "Exit" sign to the street, followed the direction I had been given to walk two blocks from the station and arrived at a massive 19th century brick building. It looked deserted. Most of the windows lining the façade were dark. I climbed the few stone steps toward a heavy wooden entrance door and was prepared for resistance. I gave it a slight push. I was surprised when it swung open easily. I walked up one flight of stairs and stepped into an empty hallway. Everything was very quiet. There was no sign of students or teachers. The helpful GI had said that the "spring term" was not to start for another two weeks or so.

Clutching the piece of paper with the number of the room in which I was to meet with the school official, I had a sinking feeling that I was heading toward nothing. That there was no room in the building with that number on the door. That even if the good soldier/angel had told the truth about having made the appointment, no one would be waiting for me. Or, if there were, the someone expecting me, would treat me to a blank stare, while out of my mouth came out a stream of clumsy babbling, trying to pass for the English language.

Putting one foot in front of the other I walked on along a hallway painted brown halfway up the wall. Above that a dingy beige took over. I arrived at a door with frosted glass panels, clearly marked with the number on the piece of paper in my hand. Before I knocked, I tried to arrange my face into what I thought was a pleasant but neutral expression. I heard a voice that might have said "come in," and opened the door.

Behind a large wooden desk with a typewriter and a telephone, stacked with books and folders of papers tightly arranged or piled on top of each other, pens and pencils nestled in a big mug printed with a picture of the Empire State Building, sat a pretty young woman with short, curly brown hair, wearing a green sweater set and a perky little color coordinated checkered scarf knotted around her neck.

She treated me to a smile, "Hello, come right in, miss....." she said.

I was surprised by the "miss." My Stockholm teachers had been strict and distant.

Excessive politesse was not accorded students in a Swedish "realskola." A hand extended toward me across the desk.

"Welcome to New York City," said my interrogator to be. "I am a student counselor in charge of admissions." So that was her title.

"My name is ...," I didn't catch it. "Please have a seat."

"Please, have a seat," surprised me. In my English, I would have expected, "please, sit down." I did. Lowering myself into one of the two wooden chairs on my side of the desk.

"Let's see what you have for us," the counselor continued.

Out of my old school bag I took out the folder of attendance records and final grades, spanning my almost completed four years in a Stockholm "realskola." The GI

had said that for this interview there was no need to bring my portfolio of artwork.
I handed the papers across the desk to the counsellor
"You have to translate," she said with a laugh. "I don't know Swedish,"
I nodded, adding what I thought was an understanding smile and said: "Yes, miss,"
I hoped that was a correct way in English to address a young high school counselor in charge of admissions to an American school.
Then, in the measured staccato march of words exiting my mouth one at a time, I began to translate and explain the subjects I had studied.
I knew that good grades in Swedish history and the Lutheran religion, would probably not count. But, I did make a case for having a grasp of elements of European history. That we had studied the Thirty Year War and the French Revolution. I added that I was somewhat familiar with the better known Shakespeare plays read in Swedish. And "Hamlet," stumbled through in the original as part of English studies.
I went on with an earnest recitation of my reading list of classic European novels, "Madame Bovary," "The Idiot," "War and Peace..."
I added that I had seen "Death of a Salesman" at the Royal Dramatic Theatre performed in Swedish. That I had read a "A Farewell to Arms" also in Swedish. And, since I was coming to New York, I had worked on reading a few Walt Whitman poems in English. I said that I knew many of August Strindberg's plays and stories. I was surprised by the counselor's nod of recognition when I mentioned "The Dwarf" by the

recent Swedish Nobel Prize winner, Pär Lagerqvist. I decided not to mention that my girlfriends and I had passed around a pirated translation of "Lady Chatterley's Lover."

The pretty, green sweatered young New York City school counselor facing me across her crowded desk, was not turning out to be the third degree interrogator I had been preparing myself for. My suspicions and fears began to loosen their grip. I was stumbling on phrases, yes, but, after listening to my litany, the counselor said that the Literature and European History studies and final math grades from my Stockholm school were acceptable.

"For all those, you will be given credit," she said.

"Credit!" A word that in my vocabulary belonged in money exchange, not in measuring of scholastic achievement.

The counselor turned to the requirements I would need to qualify for a high school diploma. She listed courses in American history and literature. She mentioned "The Scarlet Letter" and poems by Edna Saint Vincent Millay and "The Yearling." Wasn't that a book about a deer, or a horse? For children? Because I was going to take art classes, she suggested I read "Lust for Life," a brand new book about Vincent Van Gogh.

"Your English is good," said the nice young school counselor. "Obviously, it no longer counts as a foreign language. To graduate you will need credit for that." She added with a giggle: "Not Swedish."

I had come through a large chunk of the morning's challenge. Before feeling myself sliding back into my earlier fears, I jumped in:

"As you see in my school records, we were required to study German as well as English," I said quickly. "May I be allowed to take an exam in German?"

"It's not included in our requirements," said the counselor, adding after a short pause: "But, I don't see why not. I'll try to arrange it."

"We'll let you know," she added with a smile. "Soon." She reached across her crowded desk to shake my hand. "Good luck to you."

Taking her hand, I hoped my sense of relief and gratitude had not led me to squeeze or shake too hard.

Stepping out of the office back into the two-tone brownish corridor, I wasn't really sure about what I was taking away from this meeting. But I wanted to believe, that the door closing behind me was not an exit, but an entrance to a bit of promise.

2.

Three days later, in the still empty school, I was sitting at a desk, in a classroom with high ceilings and dirty windows protected with crisscrossed wire mesh. A "monitor," not at all as friendly and reassuring as the perky counselor had been, handed me sheets of mimeographed papers, with the German exam and two sharpened yellow pencils tipped with pink rubber erasers.

"You have one hour and fifteen minutes," he said, returning to his seat behind the desk in front of the blackboard. During the duration of the test he glanced up at me from behind his newspaper only now and then. That was the extent of his monitoring of the exam taking student.

There was black humor in all this. Seven years after the Allies and the United States had brought the Nazis to their knees, I sat bent over printed pieces of test papers at a gouged and ink stained wooden desk in a school room in New York City, about to come one step closer to acceptance into an American high school. By taking a for "credit" exam in a tongue that still echoed in my ears with the words of "Rauss," "Schnell..." "Verfluchte Jude,"

The test was not difficult. I translated elementary German phrases into English. English phrases into German. I conjugated basic verbs: Ich habe, du hast, sie ....etc. I answered questions: "Wie heist du?" "Ich heiss..."Was hast du? "Ich habe eine Blume." "Wo gehst du?" "Wo ist Deine Muter? Vater? Schwester? Bruder?" Wilst du etwas essen? Wo sind die Leute?"...

At the end of that section, there was one final part to complete: Write down a page of a German text you know.

For a moment I went blank. Then a rescue revealed itself. I started humming Brahms' Lullaby quietly to myself. With help of the melody, phrases of a gentler German language welled up in my memory. And, as if I were threading beads on a string one after another words began to line up: "Guten'Abend, Gut Nacht,...Mit

Rosen bedacht"...."mit Näglein, beschteckt"... and so on. My friends and I had sung it sweetly in the school choir. I wrote down the text to two verses.

The points on the two pencils were almost worn down. I was relieved that I had completed the test without the need to ask the monitor for a replacement. I had only used the pink eraser at the top of one of the pencils. I handed over the papers to the dour monitor guy at the blackboard.

And, although German did not figure as a foreign language requirement, I learned a week later that I had passed the test. I had been given "credit" for a foreign language. I was cleared for entry into an American high school in New York City.

3.

Starting in February, throughout spring, I trudged to the IRT, rode the New Lots trains uptown, downtown... I was getting used to the navigating and sounds of the noisy, rattling subway trains. The following weeks and months of school were tolerable. And not difficult. The classes that involved the reading of American story books and basic history were simple. I became a greedy collector of words, coaxing my brain into more artful clustering of expressions in the language, which was seducing me with every turn of a printed page and every overheard bit of even the tritest conversation. In speaking, American English began to replace the British inflections still clinging to my Swedish accent.

The art classes were serious. Every bit as good as the classes I had attended in the Stockholm art school. We were allowed modestly draped, however, models in life class. Our teacher was a young woman, a painter, who lived in Greenwich Village. I had learned that was the part of New York City where artists lived. Someday, I would live there, I promised myself. The school supplied canvas, paints and brushes and drawing pads. The teacher liked my paintings of heroic, strong figures in the style of Russian Revolutionary posters and drawings and paintings of still lives and flowers.

When in a year I completed the requirements for the high school diploma she helped me assemble a better organized, more impressive portfolio of my student work than the one I had carried with me from Stockholm.

I did make friends among some of the girls. But, I felt distanced from them. In Stockholm I had acquired a veneer of a confident teenager. The New York girls with their perfect teeth, their poodle skirts and crinolines and saddle shoes and their giggling conversations about Saturday nights with boyfriends they did not "go all the way" with, I found to be naïve. Still, they exuded a glow of slickness my Stockholm friends had not possessed. They stood out secure in their delineated urban universe. I was not excluded. Oh, no! I was made to feel welcome. To a fault. Taking upon themselves the mantle of American rescuers, certain what my answer would be, they often asked:

"Aren't you lucky you're here now?"

I nodded. I smiled. I left the question hanging in the air.

One Saturday afternoon, one of my new friends invited me to a New York theatre show. I was stunned by the sparkle of gilded decor, plush carpets and scintillating chandeliers of the huge lobby of the Radio City Music Hall. In my plush, sumptuous seat, I gasped when the orchestra levitated out of the pit. I loved the voluminous sound of the electric organ and the way the giant crimson curtain parted in perfect folds, revealing the line of long legged dancing girls who moved with the precision of military marching. This was my first visit to a theatrical performance since I had arrived in New York City. In Stockholm I had gone to the opera and plays and concerts, but I had never seen or heard anything so overblown and voluptuously spectacular on such a large stage, in such a glittering palace. In the seat next to mine, my classmate met the enthusiasm of her immigrant friend. with an indulgent smile.

Back in my Brooklyn tenement room, it came to me. My new New-York City school friend had intended to show this smart European arrival, who read serious books and knew languages and listened to classical music, a bit of gaudy popular Americana designed for simple tastes. My starry eyed enthusiasm did not match the image of the sophisticated European émigré I was trying to project.

4.

My father found a job in a cosmetic factory on Long Island. He took the subway to a designated spot at the Brooklyn Queens border. There he met up with a group of other workers to carpool the rest of the way.

The factory belonged to a celebrated doyenne of cosmetics. She, herself, had been a Jewish escapee from Eastern Europe. Via Paris, however. Where she had made herself and her cosmetics and perfumes well known and sought after. She had come to America with fame for her art and jewelry collections preceding her. She was good to the newly arrived, leftover Jewish immigrants.

Working in the shipping department, packing face creams and lipsticks and mascaras into neat mailing boxes, was not a taxing industrial job. Father was content working in an internationally recognized business, owned by a Jewish tycoon lady. Before the Nazis took everything, he had been a successful owner of a small candy factory in Kraków. During the years before the war, in his circle of business men, he had acquired the status of a smart wheeler dealer.

At work in the factory, he wore coveralls and shoes the union supplied, free of charge once every six months. To and from his job he camouflaged his laborer identity by changing to a suit and hat and carrying a briefcase.

At the plant my father made friends with a married couple who kept a stand at a week-end flea market. Some Saturday mornings he joined them to help selling their costume jewelry. The couple picked him up at our apartment building in their old car and drove to Lodi, New Jersey. While still dreaming of reclaiming his wheeler dealer life from before the war, he felt at home in this sort of improvised distribution of goods. Peddling was in his blood. He found satisfaction in associating with his own kind. "Nasze": one of ours, a word that belonged to my parents. In Stockholm, Sweden, there were very few "nasze." So far, on this side of the Atlantic, I couldn't get away from nasze or from family.

One Saturday my father had to work overtime at the factory. He would not be able to help his friends at the flea market. Christmas was coming.

"Zay niit help for viikent," he said. Could I take his place? "You vill yearn saam monii." I hesitated. I needed pocket money. I said "Yes."

It was still dark that Saturday morning when the doorbell rang. I threw on my coat and ran down the six flights of stairs to meet and greet the "nasze" couple, employers for the day in the front seat in their old gray car. I opened the rear door and climbed into the back seat, maneuvering myself into what room was left between the paper bags and cardboard boxes with the wares going to the flea market. I was greeted with a mumbled "good morning."

The husband and wife, in tight gray woolen coats that matched the color of their car looked shapeless squeezed into the car seat. The man wore a visored cap.

Around her head, his wife had tied a scarf babushka style. I exchanged a few words with them in English. They spoke with very heavy accents.

For most of the trip I was silent, only half listening to the couple talking to each other in Polish, here and there sprinkled with phrases in Yidisch, which I understood only now and then. I never spoke Polish anymore. The sound of the language grated on me. It seemed to have been designed for arguments. When my parents spoke with each other or their various "nasze," Polish never ceased to sound as if they were quarreling, or, at least, strongly disagreeing.

After crossing a bridge over one river and continuing on empty early morning city streets, then driving through a tiled tunnel out of New York onto a wide highway called a "turnpike," we were greeted by an official road sign: "Welcome to New Jersey." I was more than ready to be out of my cramped seat in the stuffy old car and be welcomed to New Jersey.

We arrived, in a not yet crowded parking lot, in front of a large hangar-like structure. All three of us piled out of the crowded car. The man opened the trunk. Still more boxes and bags were lifted out to add to those that had crowded me in back seat.

I helped my employers carry the stuff into the vast open space. There was bustle and noise and unpacking and setting up on folding tables and wooden planks placed on sawhorses. Near our trading spot, there was an impressive stand of pots and pans and various kitchen paraphernalia arranged on one oblong plank. On a square improvised table nearby were stacked transistor radios and gramophone records.

In a big area, on long clothes racks, women's house dresses and aprons were hung on rows and rows of wire hangers. Bras and slips and garter belts and nightgowns and flat sealed plastic wrapped packages of stockings were laid out on two improvised counters. Men's and women's shoes, arranged according to size perched in pairs on a rickety set of shelves, gaped, inviting buyers to slip their feet in. A large booth equipped with long racks of men's coats and suits had a sign marked "Dressing Room" pointing to a curtained off cubicle.

"BUY SUIT! GET SECOND PAIR PANTS FREE," announced a hand lettered placard suspended above the "dressing room."

In their designated spot, out of the paper bags and cardboard boxes, I began to help my nasze peddler couple to unwrap and lay out on their two reserved improvised stands, displays of rhinestone and imitation pearl necklaces, clip-on earrings, charm bracelets, ankle bracelets, gold plated chains with stars of David or crosses, and broaches and tiaras….

I helped arrange trinkets on scraps of velvet in small cushioned boxes and hung chains on little stands. The pieces of jewelry were priced according to size and intricacy. Not all the pieces carried visible tags with prices scribbled and attached. For those that didn't I was given a little notebook to consult.

In no time doors opened to customers. Women of all ages began to crowd and buzz around our displays with questions; "How much are these earrings?" "How much for that necklace?" "What's the price of?…"

They peered and rejected and walked away. When there was a request to try a necklace or earrings, I began to find a way to detain those who hesitated. I soon guessed whom I might be able to entice with a little bit of flattery. I had a box with tissue paper and ribbons and little paper bags for wrapping. When I did succeed in making a sale, I would present the customer with a nice little package. I took the payment, made change and stashed the money in a small tin cashbox with separate compartments for change and for bills.

About two hours into the selling morning, the whole place was milling with crowds of shoppers. A teen aged girl wearing dungarees bobbysocks and loafers, very pretty, with a short, perky blond ponytail, pointed to a charm bracelet hung with a playing card, a tiny Statue of Liberty, a half moon, a star, a baseball, and a heart with "LOVE" engraved on it. While the girl preened and turned her wrist this way and that, an older woman asked to see a matching set of a rhinestone necklace and clip-on earrings. When that led to no sale, I turned back to the young charm bracelet customer.

She had vanished. And with her the charm bracelet on her wrist! I was about to call a guard, or tell my employer. I changed my mind. Did I really care? Would it matter? My bosses hadn't noticed a thing. If I told them, they would make a stink and blame me. The girl had been smart, sneaking away like that.

I went back to smiling and enticing. I turned my attention to a customer pointing to a double strand pearl choker, a necklace that fits tightly around the throat of the wearer. Chokers looked good on young women with long necks. And hair in bouncy ponytails. The plump middle aged woman with a Mamie Eisenhower haircut topped with a veiled hat had a short stubby neck. When I helped her with the clasp, little folds of skin rippled above and below the strands of pasty beads. Holding up a small hand mirror for her, I, the salesgirl with the foreign accent said,

"It looks very nice on you, madame,.. " I could tell she liked being addressed as "madame."

When the woman looking into the mirror hesitated I went on in a confidential whisper, "I saw the exact same necklace at Orbach's last week for $14.98." I made a split second decision to not tell the prospective buyer that, here and now, at this stand, the price not visibly tagged but clearly marked in my little book, was $6.98.

"Our price is only $9.98,"I said.

Embarrassed by caving to a bit of temptation, the shopper giggled, "I guess I'll treat myself."

"Would you like to wear it?" I asked.

No, she preferred to save her necklace for a special occasion. I liked her. I unclasped the necklace, wrapped it in tissue paper, and dropped it into a little paper bag. Before tying a ribbon around the package, I winked and included a pair of small matching clip-ons without charge. The woman reached into her handbag for her wallet and counted out ten dollars. One five dollar bill and five ones. I placed the money in the cash box and gave my customer her two cents change.

As soon as I thought it safe, I helped myself to three one dollar bills and tucked them into the right hand pocket of my homemade gathered skirt that I had sewn from fabric bought in a store on Delancey Street.

And, so, whenever Mr. and Mrs. nasze in Lodi, New Jersey on the East Coast of the United States of America, busy with their own enticing and selling and paying not much attention to me, I, the hired help, did a brisk peddling of shiny trinkets, charging the slightly higher price I decided on at the spur of the moment. The legitimate sum went in the metal box and the rest was slid into my skirt pocket.

I was just making change for a woman who had bought a gold plated chain ankle bracelet, while simultaneously telling a tall man with a crew cut, in army fatigues, the price, my price, of a pair of rhinestone chandelier earrings he was holding up, when I noticed that the earrings had a tag with a price clearly marked.

"That's not what it says here," the man said. He seemed ready for battle. "This price here says,...." My lady boss heard and intervened.

"Ach, ja!" she said. "Sorry mister,..."nue girrl make mistake...Sorrry"...

"I am so sorry, sir" I mumbled. "I did make a mistake," I turned to my boss and said I was sorry.
The soldier bought the earrings. After giving me a dirty look, he made a point of handing the money to my employer. I watched him strut away and get lost in the crowd. My nasze lady opened the lid and cast a quick glance at the money collecting in the cash box I was in charge of. It was filling up. She saw that the jewelry on the velvet cloths and on the little wire stands was moving along. I was obviously doing my job, selling well.

I gave in to a brief moment of panic. It passed. But, for the next hour or so, I was careful to check if there was a visible price tag attached to the piece of jewelry that a customer may be contemplating. I consulted the price in the notebook. When asked, I quoted it clearly. *Viva voce*. When I was sure that my bosses were occupied, each busy with a customer, I went back to my creative adjustments.

Even though they did not offer to treat me, my employers let me have a break for lunch. I was sorry I hadn't thought of bringing a sandwich. I did a turn around the crowded, noisy space, stopping briefly by the shoe display. I was skillful at making my clothes, but shoes were another story. It would have been nice to slip into a pair of black patent leather pumps with graceful medium high heels. Here they would be cheaper than a pair in a regular shoe store. I felt for the money in my pocket. I probably had enough, but decided it was not a good idea to flaunt it.

At a food stand, I felt for coins in my pocket, fishing out a couple of quarters to pay for a frankfurter with mustard and a bottle of Coca Cola. Nothing suspicious about having brought lunch money with me. I found a bench in a deserted corner away from the busy stands and sat down to eat my lunch. Then, at the end of the big hall I found a bathroom. I was glad that it was empty. I peed, washed my hands.

The face of the girl looking back at me from the smudged glass of the mirror was angry. At her mother. At her father. At herself. For having said "yes" to this job. For having said "yes" to leaving Sweden. For having said "yes" to coming to America.

In Stockholm, during my last summer, before I even knew that it was to be my last summer, I had a job in the city's big, elegant department store. Tourist travel from America and Canada was only just beginning to trickle to Sweden. Salesclerks with some knowledge of English were needed. Behind a mahogany counter and glass displays, I assisted two prim and proper older ladies, sisters, who had worked there forever, selling fine Belgian lace. I had loved the elegance of that job. The two sisters liked me. When, just before my departure from Stockholm, I went to say a tearful goodbye to them, they presented me with a beautiful lace collar as a farewell present.

How had I ended up in a world that bore no resemblance to that salesgirl behind a mahogany counter with polished glass display cases. Or to the Technicolor vision of Hollywood films that my friends and I had rushed to as soon as they played in one of our local movie theatres. The American high school students in those movies drove to school or to a dance or to a ball game in their own fancy cars.

On this Saturday not long before Christmas, I was assisting a churlish round couple peddling tacky trinkets in broken English, at a flea market in Lodi, New Jersey, a place not far from New York Harbor, not far from the Statue of Liberty, far, far from Stockholm, Sweden,

I went back to my selling post. No threats rose up before me for the rest of my creative selling day. When time came to close up shop, I helped pack and carry the now lighter bags and boxes back to the car. When the trunk was filled, what was left would keep me company in the back seat on the return trip to Brooklyn. I handed my cash box to my bosses in the front seat.

My employers had not counted the money. Probably to avoid doing it before watchful eyes of other peddlers. When I handed the now heavier box to my nasze lady boss, I could tell she could tell by the weight, that it had turned out to be a successful selling day.

On the return trip to Brooklyn, crowded into the back seat of the little car, I should have been tired. I wasn't. I should have felt guilty. I didn't. I felt good. I thought it might have been fun to have hooked up with the ponytailed charm bracelet thief. To tell her that she had inspired me to turn the tacky job into a satisfying criminal adventure.

I recalled the times before the Nazis came, when I was a very little girl in Kraków. The times when with my hand in Niania's hand, we walked to the city's main square to the flea market. While she turned up her nose at the people who bought and sold cheap, shoddy things at the "tandeta," she knew I thought the displays of gaudy artificial paper flowers, shiny baubles and ribbons were beautiful. Once she did buy me a piece of an embroidered blue ribbon for my hair.

"Many bad thieves come here to steal things," Niania would tell me. "They run and get lost in the crowd."

Then we would go inside Kościój Maryacki. Niania, wrapped her rosary around her fingers. I listened to her whispering her prayers "Ave Maria, Gratia Plena, Dominus...." I learned to whisper the Latin words along with her. I looked at the pictures of the Christ child and the Virgin and saints and angels on the walls of the church. I loved the smell of incense lingering after the last mass. I loved the light streaming through the stained glass windows. Sometimes there was organ music playing. I loved being in church with Niania even more than looking around at colorful stuff at the "tandeta."

In Brooklyn my bosses for the day delivered me back to my building. I was surprised by the smiles and handshakes I was treated to by the otherwise dreary couple. They thanked me for my help and paid me fifteen dollars for the day's work. I added the respectably earned salary to the wad of secret dollar bills and coins nestling in the right hand pocket of my skirt. Before the door to my building closed behind me I waved good-bye to the couple in the departing car.

Later in my room I counted my loot. Altogether it came to $57.80.

"You solt goot," my father said after he had reconnected with his nasze at work the following Monday."Zay vant you shoult come back."

When, two weeks later, the couple asked my father if I could come help with sales at the Lodi tandeta once again, I didn't dare say "yes."

"I can't, I have too much reading for school for Monday" I said. "And, a painting that I have to finish."

From black and white crime movies I had learned, that the bad guys were often lured to repeat the success of their scams. It seldom worked. They usually got caught.

5.

After the surprise of the much milder winter than I had been used to in Stockholm, I was not prepared for the brutality of the heat of the New York City summer. Swedish summers had been cool and glowing, short and precious. With long, long sunny days, followed by nights that only visited during a few short hours of teasing darkness. How I came to miss that clean, sparkling air in the heaving and churning summer days and nights of the New York metropolis.

I got a summer job in a doll factory. The workplace was stacked with cardboard boxes filled with parts of dolls. Torsos and arms and legs and heads waited to be assembled and dressed. These rubber disembodiments emitted an insistent, fetid smell. They were unpleasant to the touch.

We worked assembly style at long tables. My job was inserting a creaky tin turntable into the belly and testing the device by tilting the doll backwards. If it worked, the doll yammered, "mommy, mommy, pick me up."

A half-hour was allowed for lunch, two fifteen minutes breaks for coffee. The heat and lack of any ventilation was the main topic of conversation. The whirring of a couple of giant fans made a lot of noise but did little to move air. There were many such small factories aptly named "sweatshops," which manufactured clothes, small leather goods, hats, household goods..... all over the city.

To complete yet another requirement toward my diploma, three evenings a week, I attended a high school course called "Economics." I listened to insistent facts about antitrust laws and ironclad statements regarding "bad money driving, out good money" by an instructor who droned on and on about, "Free trade and individual freedom, is what America is about, folks." Saying this, he seemed to be focusing on me and another couple of new arrivals from abroad.

"Folks" with its redundant "s" attached to the word at the end, grated on me. The word "folk" in Swedish, meant "the people." In German it had the same meaning. But, "Das Deutsche Volk" had been sullied by its Nazi reference to exclusive Aryan purity.

Trapped in this ugly classroom, harshly lit with neon light bulbs, again with a useless fan whirring in the back of the room, it took an effort to concentrate on the blather coming from our heavyset pompous teacher with the razor thin part in his brilliantined slicked down, mousy brown hair and the sweat stains on his seersucker jacket showing every time he raised an arm to write on the black board. I hoped to retain just enough of what he was spewing at us in my head, and in notes I dutifully scribbled in my notebook, to get through the exam at the end of the summer.

Among the pleasures I had left behind in Stockholm was my sunny, sexy romance with a blond Swedish boy I had met at a club for Communist Youth. We used to go to readings of translations of Russian classics and screenings of movies together. One evening we attended a screening of a modern day movie adaptation of "Romeo and Juliet." In it the young lovers were workers at a machine plant in Odessa. The plot was reinterpreted to serve propaganda. Nevertheless, the couple could not escape the traditional tragic ending.

On that beautiful evening in Stockholm, the moon was full. Its double shimmered on the waters of Lake Mälaren. Both seemed to smile at us. We did not yet know that I would soon be heading west across the waters of the Atlantic Ocean.

In letters to my friends, I was too ashamed to admit that my life in America was nothing like the life of high school students in the American Technicolor musicals. I lied and embroidered my writing with tales of the many social events I was often invited to.

After a year I got sick of making up these stories about dances and "garden parties" and my thin Par Avion letters flying across the Atlantic became less and less frequent. So were the responses from Stockholm. I began to make an effort to stop my longing and lamenting for the gentle airy city and the life in it that would never again be mine.

Would a time ever come for me to get in step with the raucous whirl and daunting vigor of this huge American city I had been tossed into against my will? So far, New York only teased me with a distant promise that might take me away from sweaty days spent stuffing screechy gadgets into the innards of ugly rubber dolls. And evenings spent in a neon lit classroom listening to a sweating man, trying to stuff me full of inane propaganda veiled as economics instruction. It was not easy to try to open myself up to the contemplation of the elegant, witty stalk of the Empire State Building, tickling the sky, visible from so many angles of the city. Or, give myself to delighting in the span and arches of the miracle of the Brooklyn Bridge. It was not easy to have the patience to wait for a door to open on a life that would be more than the next ride on a crowded, clattering subway train in the black underground hole to and from my tenement.

After work and night class, there was not much relief waiting for me in the airless sixth floor tenement room with speckled linoleum floor and window facing a dingy airshaft. I had my small easel, a desk for doing homework, and an old foot pedaled Singer sewing machine we had carried from Stockholm. Along with other bits and pieces of furniture my parents had picked up in various secondhand stores, they had found an old cabinet radio. It was a large piece of beat-up furniture, which took up space in one corner of my little room. But it worked! I was surprised and happy to have come upon the one station that played classical music for many hours of the day and evening.

Often, even during the most stifling summer nights, the heating pipes and the radiators in the building kicked in without warning, spewing smells of gas and corroded iron. I would wake up gasping for air and bathing in sweat.

One of those nights there was a pause in the symphonic music broadcast. The airwaves were thick with the news of the Rosenberg executions. Their crime had to do with selling atomic secrets to Communist Russia. The officious radio voices reported the last minute refusals of pleas for stays of execution. Over and over. Until all the attempts were exhausted. The condemned husband and wife were allowed to say goodbye to their two young sons.

I pictured the doomed couple being taken together to the execution chambers. Or were they to be led away separately? Who would be the first? Would there be a need to cut the collars of their prison garb the way the traitors in the past were prepared for the guillotine's blade? Would that be a redundancy in the modern day jolt of electricity? Would the Rosenbergs be strapped into two electric chairs placed side by side like twin marriage beds. Would the lethal electrical dose be turned on at the same time? If the doomed needed restraining were more than one executioner to be on hand? Were they trained to be polite as they went about their work.

The next morning, in the wire service photos, looking like so many faces in crowds of recent nameless victims in Germany and Poland, the Jewish faces of the betrayers of the USA stared at the world from the front pages of the world's newspapers.

"Aren't you lucky you're here now!"

LATER

Cups and Saucers

1.

The spring I had been married to my art school sweetheart for two years, we lived in an apartment on the top floor of a four story walk-up in the Fort Greene section of Brooklyn not far from the art school where we had met as students.

The apartment had two small rooms, a kitchenette area, a bathroom. What had been our bedroom for a time, we turned into a room for our baby girl. We painted funny figures of people and animals and garlands of flowers in her room not only for the amusement of our baby, but also to disguise the many cracks and bulges in the wall.

We bought a sofa bed for the living room. Every night the machinery screeched when it was opened and unfolded to become the marriage bed. The atonal tune recurred in reverse when we folded the contraption, making of it a sofa for daytime use. Two windows offered a view of a small backyard. There was a catalpa tree that reached its leafy branches all the way to our fourth floor window in the summer. In the fall, when the tree lost its leaves, it grew ugly, curving brown pods, we could hear plopping down onto the asphalt in the backyard.

"They look like shriveled penises," my husband would observe.

Our pretty baby girl had bright, dark eyes and masses of black curly hair. Our life was simple. We needed very little. There was time to draw and paint. I had good training under my belt. We both did. I was determined that the things I had learned in art school and from fellow art students might lead to paying work at some point. I missed my girlhood in Stockholm but, kept sweeping such thoughts aside.

My husband was witty and loving. He had strong, square shoulders and grey eyes, which twinkled behind heavy horn rimmed glasses. During the day he had a job as a sign painter. I liked that. That made us part of the proletariat. That satisfied my socialist/communist "workers arise" beliefs. In my innocent, wedded, cozy life, filled with daily domestic routines, I still clung to the ideals and loyalties carried with me from my cliques of young Communists in Sweden. It was not a time for loudly proclaiming far left loyalties in the USA. We both painted and worked on drawings at night.

I did not aspire to owning a house in the suburbs, or having an oversize automobile weighted with chrome and excessive tailfins. I tried to teach myself to become a proper cook. On my old Singer I made my own and our little girl's dresses. If my marriage to a kindred spirit and a good artist did not explode with roman candles, it was affectionate and romantic. And proper.

Our neighborhood had a convenient A&P supermarket, a newsstand on the corner, a small laundromat, to which I dragged our wash no more than once a week. On nice days I wheeled my baby in her carriage to a nearby park. While she slept, I sat on a bench, sketched in a notebook, read novels by D.H. Lawrence, Jean Paul Sartre and anything and everything by Albert Camus. I longed to take courses in French.

One sunny morning, during a week-end stroll my husband and I stopped to look at a shop that sold old used things. There were a couple of these brocanteurs in the neighborhood, junk stores, really, in which a new household with meager means could find a silver plated candlestick, a ceramic flower pitcher, a still usable picture frame, a copper sauce pan that only needed a bit of good polishing to be restored.

The store actually had "Antiques" painted in an old cursive type script at the center of the window. There were some books with old bindings placed in a small case. One book was opened to a page showing an old engraving of a man engulfed in flames. The book was printed in German Gothic script. An old gilt watch fob and a couple of broaches set with garnets and rhinestone earrings were nestled in several worn looking blue or green velvet lined cases. Some faux pearl or diamond necklaces were hung from plaster cast hands or around the necks of detached mannequin heads from the late thirties.

In the center of the window, on a polished metal tea tray covered with a doily, were displayed two pretty porcelain cups decorated with delicate tiny roses and daisies and a gold boarder around the rim. The same pattern was repeated on the saucers.

"Look at those beautiful cups!" I said to my husband. "Do you mind if, we go in and take a closer look?"

"Why not?" he smiled and picked up our sleeping baby. "We are in need of some additions to our china tea set collection." I loved my husband.

The store was dark. At first we couldn't even see the owner where he sat at a desk in the back of the store. He was an elderly man with a trim, short gray beard. His thick horn rimmed glasses had slipped half way down his nose. He wore an old fashioned brimmed cap. Pulled way up above his middle, which could no longer be called a waist, his pants were held up by suspenders. His checkered shirt was somewhat rumpled. But cuffs and collar were neatly buttoned. I thought he looked like an old style revolutionary.

The store owner smiled at us and put the book he had been reading down on the desk in front of him. I was curious to see what he was reading. I am always curious to see what people are reading. But, because the lighting was so dim in the back of the store, and the reader had placed the book with pages facing up, there was no way I could read the text on the pages or the title in small print at the top. While the antique store owner went to the window I thought of quickly turning the book around to sneak a look. But, the man was already coming back, maneuvering his bulky frame between all the stands and cases of bric-a-brac. He put the tray with the cups and saucers in front of us on his desk next to his book.

"Sèvres," he said. "Very fine French china." I was not surprised.

"How much are you asking for the set," my husband asked.

"I can't let them go for less than 25 dollars," was the response.

My husband and I exchanged a quick look. We each knew what the other one was thinking. Spending 25 dollars on a couple of porcelain cups to drink coffee out of at our foldable dinette table was a shameful unattainable frivolity.

After a slight pause my husband said, "Thank you. My wife and I will have to think about this."

"Yes," I added. "Thank you. Very much."

We made our way back to the door. The owner walked right behind us with the tray and the Sèvres china.

Outside, on the street, we put our still sleeping baby back in the carriage. The brocanteur replaced the tray with the cups and saucers in his store window. He sent us a "good-bye" wave. Which we returned before walking away.

"I don't think we need to 'think about it,'" I said.

On the short walk back to our apartment, the baby woke up and began one of the gurgle recitals that put smiles on her parents' faces. I was still curious about the name of the big fat tome our Antiques store owner was reading.

I did not mention the cups again. But I couldn't stop thinking about them. A couple of times during the next week, with my sleeping baby in her carriage, I walked by the store. The cups were still in the window.

Then, one evening, after we had put the baby to bed, after she had stopped crying and had fallen asleep, my husband kissed me on the nose.

"I want you to have those cups," he said. "Let's see if we can't scrape the money together."

In my old tin coffee can in which I saved quarters, and only quarters, I was surprised to find six dollars and seventy five cents. In the pocket of a sweater hanging in the closet, I found two forgotten dollar bills. And, one quarter. At that time in our lives, when each dime and nickel was accounted for, it was rare for such a sum of money to have been overlooked in the pocket of a garment. I took it as a sign. After that, every time I had a quarter in change, I plopped it into the can. At the end of that week, I had amassed twelve dollars and fifty cents.

I cooked a thick soup full of potatoes and onions and white beans and barley. For several evenings dinner was "stone soup." We ate it with rye bread from Entenmanns's. Another four dollars and fifty cents was saved from grocery expenses. At the end of that week, I checked the "Antiques" store window. The cups and saucers were not only still there. It was obvious that they had not been touched since the owner had put them back in the window.

On payday Friday evening, my husband counted out eight dollars from his pay envelope. Added to my savings, old and new, we had our 25 dollars to buy me a set of two Sèvres cups and saucers.

Saturday morning we made love. My husband did. I can't say I participated with much interest. I was waiting for the moment we would walk out of the apartment, down the four flights of stairs, put our baby in the carriage kept in a nook of the so called vestibule, and turn the corner to the street where, in the shop with the word "Antiques" spelled on its window, an old gentleman, who wore suspenders and read a thick book, would hand over to me two cups and their saucers, painted with delicate flowers and gold borders by the hand of a skilled decorative artist in a porcelain factory in Sèvres, France.

The baby woke up. I changed her diaper, warmed her bottle and put her in the folded out sofa bed with her father. I showered and dressed.

At last came the moment when the three of us actually headed for the shop.

"Look," I laughed, when we arrived at the store window. "Those cups and saucers are beginning to look like they have sprouted roots in this window display."

"Well, then, time has come to uproot them," my husband said. "You go ahead and do it."

I opened the door and walked alone into the shop. I turned and smiled at my husband. He gave me an encouraging wave of the hand. It was a beautiful sunny day.

My daughter's little head in the white cap I had sewn and edged with lace, was peeking over the rim of the baby carriage. How lucky I was! I had a good, smart husband. I had a baby who smelled of talcum powder and almonds. And, I was about to acquire a pair of beautiful cups and saucers, which may have been the remainder of a tea service that had belonged to Marie Antoinette.

"I have come to buy the Sèvres cups and saucers."

I held out my change purse as if to prove to the storeowner that I actually had the cash to complete this transaction.

"I think the set has been waiting for you," the "Antiques" store man said and smiled. That was nice. It surprised me.

He had on the same baggy pants held up with suspenders. But this time, as if he may have sensed that, he was going to participate in an elegant transaction he was wearing a neatly pressed white shirt. He got up from his chair behind the desk, walked to the window, and came back carrying the tray.

I watched him wrap the two Sèvres cups and their saucers separately in pages of "The Brooklyn Eagle." He put the four wrapped pieces of china in a brown paper bag. I took the bills and the coins out of my small coin purse and handed the antique storeowner his payment. While he counted the money, I threw a quick glance at the book he had put down on his desk. It was definitely the same one he had been reading the first time we had walked into the store. He only had a small number of pages left to read. This time, he had placed the book with the cover up. I was able to read the title. It was not, as I had imagined, a Russian classic, or a revolutionary manifesto, but "Marjorie Morningstar," the best seller every hausfrau and high school girl in America was reading at the time.

I carried the carefully wrapped, coveted acquisition out into the sunshine and soft air of mid-morning. My husband pushed the baby carriage. We stopped at the A&P and bought a glazed Sara Lee coffee cake. Back home, in our top floor walk-up, I took the four bundles out of the brown paper bag and carefully freed the cups and saucers from the crinkled newspaper wrappings. I rinsed the cups and saucers under running water in the kitchen sink and dried them in a freshly laundered kitchen towel. I took the cake out of the box and put it on the nice decorative glass plate that had been a wedding present. On the dinette table, I laid two white linen placemats and matching napkins. I put plates on the place mats and added desert forks and coffee spoons. I put our new cups and saucers to the right of the plates.

In the center of the table I put, the little pitcher of flowers I had made a watercolor sketch of earlier that week. My husband looked at my wifely preparations with an amused and affectionate smile.

I measured ground coffee out of a Nedicks can into the perforated top of the tin coffeepot. I filled it with water, fitted the cover on top, lit the gas with a kitchen match and placed it on the stove burner to boil. Soon the coffee percolated and filled our place with an inviting fresh smell.

I cut two slices of the Sara Lee cake and put a slice on each plate.

"Come," I said to my husband; "Coffee and cake are being served."

I tilted the pot to pour coffee into my husband's cup and heard the crack. Before I was able to arrive at the enormity of disbelief and face the split second of what I knew had taken place, time stopped and wrapped me in a chokehold. What had happened wasn't at all complicated. In front of me, the simple fact of it was staring me in the face. The glass dome of the metal coffee pot had loosened, detached itself, crashed into the delicate little cup and broken it in half. Not much coffee had poured out of the spout, but what splattered out of the cracked two halves of porcelain barely missed burning my husband's right hand. A brown stain began to form on the white linen placemat.

At first, I was unable to make any sound. Then out of my throat, came a shapeless howl, which changed into a hysterical laugh. I threw the coffee pot with the coffee into the kitchen sink. That made a huge clattering noise. The baby, who had been peacefully sucking on her bottle, started to scream. Both of us were screaming.

My husband tried to calm us.

"Now, hush, stop this screaming, you two, hush…! It's not the end of the world," he said, adding, "Look, the cup broke into two perfect pieces. I'll be able to fix it."

I whimpered and stared at the ruin of the treasure that I had believed had meant to be mine.

"I'll go to the hardware store…" my husband continued to reassure me. "I'll ask for some strong glue. I am sure it'll work You'll see!"

A little later my husband did step out to a nearby hardware store and returned with a tube of glue. He placed a rag on the dinette table and with fingers covered with horrid, quickly drying glue, was able to join together the two broken halves of the Sèvres cup.

The pieces held. The brownish red line of glue could never be disguised.

I began to believe that those cups and saucers had, indeed, belonged, if not to Marie Antoinette herself, then to some aristocrat, whose head had fallen under the blade of the guillotine. The dried glue line on the pearly china was the color of coagulated blood. It made me think of the thin red ribbons, worn around necks by European nobility to express sympathy with French aristocrats, whose heads had been severed from their bodies during the Terror.

I was also sure that with my willful desire to posses those seductive little pieces of French china, I had unleashed a curse that may have slumbered within them.

I put the cups and saucers in the darkest recess of the kitchen cabinet. I never wanted to use even the cup that had not broken. I never used the saucers. When we moved out of that apartment a year later, I left the cups and saucers right where I had put them that morning.

LATER STILL

HOUSE

1.

The incentive to cross the street that morning began with a visit from our landlady, who had dropped in the afternoon of the day before.

Celia and her husband lived in the lower duplex of the two family house they owned. Our family occupied the third and fourth floors.

We were four now. Our son's birth was reasonably timed, three years after that of his sister. The boy arrived with a full head of red hair. It grew to be thick and luxuriant. On the street admiring passersby often stopped to bend down to ask him,

"Where did you get that gorgeous red hair?"

Once, when he couldn't have been much older than four, he surprised me with a stoic and sober answer: "It came with the head," he informed the woman who asked.

Over coffee and chitchat, our landlady had begun to grumble about an upcoming increase to New York City water charges.

"You know, what that means," she said. "Real estate taxes will go up."

Even though this information did not go any further, I imagined "RENT INCREASE," spelled out in a comic strip balloon hovering over Celia's head for the rest of the little visit.

Actually, we had been on friendly terms all through the years we had been Celia's and her husband's renters. They were a frugal couple. One could say borderline skinflints. Still, our reasonable rent held steady. During our seven years as renters there had been no increases.

Celia was serious about consciousness raising, commitment to community and family values. There was not a problem in this world which could not be solved with civic action and the adhering to Jewish customs. And psycho therapy. My defense was existential attitudes and a study of everything French. I never scored any points with Celia. What was to win?

At the end of her drop-in visit, as she was leaving, Celia let slip;

"By the way did you know, that the young couple across the street have put their house up for sale?"

No, we didn't know that. She also happened to know the asking price.

There was no reason to believe that Celia was indulging in anything but gossipy neighborhood information. She could not have imagined, that when she went back down the stairs to her part of the four story house, she had invaded the minds of her longtime renters with a powerful new thought. My husband and I looked at each and knew that we would look up the phone number and make the call to the owners of the house across the street.

On our side of the street, the two family dwellings with uniform, mostly flat facades with Tudor style accents, were row houses built during the 1920s The upper duplex we were renting was roomy, sunny, with a roof terrace reached from our bedroom/studio on the fourth floor. In the summer the space was shaded by the tops of leafy trees. Looking down, we had pleasant views of mostly neat neighboring backyards and gardens.

The houses facing us across the other side of the wide street were built during the penultimate decade of the 19th century by skilled Italian architects and masons. Each house was unique, featuring elegant and elaborate varieties of brick, marble and limestone details. From our living room window seat, on the third floor level of Celia's house, for as long as we had been her renters, we had admired the house that she happened to mention was for sale.

The morning after the coffee klatch with our landlady we walked in the middle of the street to the others side. It occurred to me that in the several years we had lived on this Park Slope Street, we had only ever crossed the street at the corners where there were lights. And now, here we were jaywalking. We hesitated in front of the house.

"Are we really doing it?" I reached for my husband's hand.

"Don't be silly," he whispered. "Of course we are.

He squeezed my hand and added, "Don't be nervous."

We walked side by side through the space, which kept the house at a decent distance from the sidewalk. There was a working gaslight surrounded by evergreens. We walked up the limestone stairs to the front door, which was flanked by two urns with green and red aspidistra plants and rang the doorbell. There was a buzz and we stepped through the outer door into the vestibule. The second door opened. We were greeted by the very pretty redhead we sometimes observed from the distance of our ample window perch. An adorable little girl was clinging to her mother's knees. We introduced ourselves. If Susie had ever been aware of us on her side of the street, she didn't say. What she did say right away was that she and her husband were handling the sale of their house themselves, without the involvement of a broker.

"I like that," my husband said. I agreed. A seller who could do without a conventional real estate broker. For some reason, I thought it was a good omen. The little girl treated the strangers to a shy smile.

Susie and her husband Jay, an attorney, had relocated to New York City from Philadelphia when he was offered an important position with the Power Authority. They had needed to find a place to live quickly. They liked their Park Slope house. But, they were selling, Susie said, chiefly because she wanted to move to Manhattan to be closer to dance and acting classes and auditions.

A few years before, she had been chosen Miss Philadelphia. There were glamorous studio shots and newspaper photographs of her posing with the mayor and local city dignitaries displayed throughout the house.

The huge window in the living room, topped with a semicircle of Tiffany style leaded stained glass with light streaming through, seemed more imposing indoors than it did from the street. There had once been a sliding door, now removed, between the living and dining room, making of the area an uninterrupted, continuous space. The original wall and ceiling patisseries, which we knew had been a staple of these houses, had been stripped. Susie had the walls in both rooms papered in woven grass cloth. Beige wall-to-wall carpeting covered the floor of the living and dining room. It felt nice under foot but it was bland. The décor of the house, proper and polite to a fault, collided with the jarring presence of a bare light bulb dangling from an exposed electrical wire above the dining room table. The kitchen was an extension, built onto the house sometime during the late 50ties. It was tucked away discreetly, hardly visible from the dining room. It had new appliances, but it was small, with odd angles, altogether unexceptional. Not a cook's kitchen.

The expanse of wall-to-wall beige carpet continued on the stairs leading up to the second floor. Here the fine parquet floors in the bedrooms had been left bare. The master bedroom facing the street was wider than the living room. It extended to the end wall of the house above the space taken up by the vestibule, entrance hall and a deep closet downstairs. Two medium sized windows were also topped with semicircles of leaded stained glass. The center motifs were red rosettes, green ribbons and laurel leaves.

"In the afternoon the sunlight streams in here," Susie said. "Rainbow colors dance on the floor. Don't they, sweetie?" The little girl began to twirl around. Her mother and we, the admiring prospective buyers, laughed and applauded.

A passageway with mirrored closets separated the master bedroom from a second large bedroom facing the back yard. I looked at my husband, silently questioning if this parade of floors, windows, and doors we were projecting into our future was having the same dizzying effect on him as it had on me.

We continued up to the third floor. Here the big room above the master bedroom had oak floors in fine condition, stained a rich dark brown and buffed with polyurethane. Three windows, were smaller than the two on the bedroom floor below. Still, the room was flooded with midmorning light. The walls were lined with inbuilt bookcases. Across the hall, two small bedrooms faced the back yards. The door to one of these rooms appeared to be stuck.

Susie apologized, saying, "That will be taken care of, of course." They had never needed the room as a bedroom, she explained. It had been mostly used for storage.

"It is the reversed version of the other room next to it," she said.

We peeked into that room. Nice. Cozy. It had a large window with a view of the top of a tree in the backyard.

All through the tour of the house my husband and I were treating Susie to admiring remarks. In my head I was redecorating.

We went back downstairs to the parlor floor. I looked beyond pretty Susie's beige grass cloth wall coverings and the matching beige wall-to-wall carpeting. I wondered what kind of floor was hidden underneath. I also wondered what the thick glossy white enamel lavished on the mantelpiece in the dining room was covering. Susie did notice that I had cast a look at the bare light bulb dangling on an electrical wire above the dining table.

"Oh, we never found just the right fixture," she laughed.

"This is a very beautiful house," I said. "It feels like a lucky house."

"I agree," my husband said, "It's a perfect house." He turned to me and winked.

There was a basement apartment, which had been the original kitchen and servant's quarters. "It needs some work," Susie admitted. We took a quick look. It was dark. It had been used or rented out over the years by the previous owners of the house. Susie had no information about any of that. She said that she and Jay had kept it for storage. Which is what the place looked like to us. An attic below stairs.

"We didn't feel like being landlords," Susie said.

Not like Celia, I thought. Who seemed born to be a landlady!

I took one last look up at the high living room ceiling. I looked toward the dining room and the bare light bulb. The end of the tour on the way out the surprising rapport we had established with the charming young seller led to warm embraces with her and the little girl. We made arrangements to return for drinks in the afternoon to meet with husband Jay when he came home from the office. For now, there was nothing much to be added.

Feeling giddy, shaken and stunned by the whole improbable experience we had propelled ourselves into, my husband and I went back to our rented duplex, settled into the third floor living room window and looked back to where we had just come from. Until this moment the house across the street had been for us a piece of fine, almost century old urban domestic architecture to feast our eyes on. We had been tourists admiring the scenery. This morning we had stepped behind the façade, penetrated the interior and were now looking back toward the thing from which we had just returned, overwhelmed with a mad, tingling desire to possess.

It was early spring. April. The leaves on the big trees lining this wide Park Slope street had not yet burst into the later heaviness that would obstruct the view.

It seemed as if the house had drawn an outline around itself that had not been there before. It appeared to have detached itself and taken a step forward, to take a bow, to continue the introduction, and with a wink, was inviting us to caress the lines and volumes of its edifice up and down and sideways. To admire the fine proportions of delicate horizontal stripes and arrangements of red brick and grey and white stone. To let us follow the curved form of a fan shape around the big Palladian first floor window. To emphasize how above the heavy oak frame of the double glass entrance door, the various colors of stone and brick formed a design that resembled the curve of a woman's decorative hair ornament. Cradling the two semicircular windows, with the "dancing rainbow color" stained glass so vividly reflecting on the bedroom floor, were columns built of brick and set slightly forward from the wall. Our gaze moved up toward the three marble columns supporting the ledge of the third floor lintel. Depending on weather and time of day the limestone and red brick seemed always to be at play with light and shade.

"Look at those three windows on the top floor," said my husband. "That will be our studio." Under the roof extension nestled a frieze of finely carved acanthus. We hugged. He kissed me on the nose.

Nothing had really happened yet. We had only said to the pretty seller that we loved her house and expressed our seriousness as prospective buyers. But as soon as we left her and her little girl and crossed the street back to our apartment, we had both been overcome with shudders of excitement and terror. Not even twenty four hours had passed since Celia had sipped coffee at the table in our rented dining room of her house. Now here we were, sitting in the window seat we didn't own, but had made our own, letting our desires fly toward the elegant marble and brick temptation, winking at us, inviting us into its embrace of spacious rooms and large windows. We were giving in to a seduction we had no intention resisting.

"It does look different than it did before," said my husband.

"It must sense that something is going to change within its walls," I said.

2.

My husband and I had never looked at a house to buy. We had lived in and moved from smaller to larger apartments. We paid rent. We arranged furniture and books. We worked and ate and slept in the rented rooms we lived in. Owning houses was for other people. And yet...here we were.

There followed somewhat less giddy, more practical, still very convivial meetings with Susie and Jay. When the time came to sign the preliminary contract, my husband and I had juggled some funds and were ready with a bank check to be held in escrow.

"Escrow." A snappy but weighty word that had never resided in the vicinity of my vocabulary. And the climb into property ownership continued. We met with a lawyer, an inspection engineer, a title searcher. We were told to make a call to an insurance company.

"You can transfer your renters' insurance," said the agent I talked to.

We had no renters' insurance. We had never thought of such a thing. We signed up for house insurance and put a check in the mail. With every new necessity that had to be properly lined up, and put in place, we felt not unlike little kids who enjoyed scaring themselves.

"What are we doing?" I looked to my husband for reassurance.

"Grownup things," he said.

"Oh," I said. "So, that's how that works."

A few days after our leap into putting our house buying in motion, I ran into Celia at Key Foods.

"You know, the house across the street found buyers already," she said.

"I know," I said. "We are buying it."

There are times in life when an unexpected moment leading to an opportunity to deliver a simple mundane phrase, leads to rewarding one with an overwhelming and disproportionate sense of triumph. A movie trailer of my early days in New York, my dreary tenement room, the parade of make-do apartments my husband and I had made livable for ourselves and our children, screened in my head. And the gleeful thought of my intellectual one-upmanship attempts to score points with Celia that had come to naught. Well, moving to the good side, to ownership of a house on the status side of the street, was a coup.

Unloading two bags of groceries on the table of the soon to be vacated kitchen in the duplex apartment, I said to my husband,

"Now, we can tell Celia that she will be able to roll over the water charges to her new renters."

"I am sure she needs no counseling from us," he laughed. "Raising the rent on new tenants will make her little landlady heart pitter-patter faster."

And so, my husband and I continued to have a great time playing with the scenarios the house acquisition was opening up to us. There was no logic in our victory, but our reveling in it was boundless.

Our incomes had been steadily growing. My husband had ceased to be a proletarian sign painter when he moved, at first tentatively, then smartly, into a steady success in writing and illustrating picture books. After exit from art school, I had fallen into designing textiles for dress fabrics and wallpapers for several years. Then, my husband's perceptive and enthusiastic young editor saw a promise in the blooms and figurines and playful elements within my designs. She encouraged me to follow in my husband's footsteps into illustrating, and writing, picture books. I soon made a discovery. When I first thought of being a painter, I imagined making large, dramatic, theatrical works. By shrinking those images I transformed the scale of murals into miniatures. I fell into something that liked me well. By the time of the jump into fancy house buying and mortgage applications, I had written and/or illustrated several picture books.

The PR of a married couple working in books for children, played well with publishers and book buyers and librarians. I kept a door opened to my designing of fabrics and wallpapers. Sales happened sporadically or un, deux, trois. I acted in plays off and off-off Broadway. That brought little or no money. I sometimes got cast in commercials, which did. We never lacked for work. Still, it was a freelance income. It was surprising that we had no trouble being approved for a mortgage.

At the closing, surrounded with lawyers and bank loan officials, we and the soon to be former owners sat facing each other on opposite sides of a conference table. Papers were signed and checks passed back and forth. There was affability and beginnings and endings. After lunch at a restaurant at The Waldorf, we exchanged hugs with the sellers with whom we had become quite friendly. They had moved on to the elegant gem of a little house on Bedford street, in the West Village that had once belonged to a famed couple of opera singers.

My husband and I rushed back to Park Slope, climbed the front steps, between the vivid potted greenery, entered the little vestibule paved in small mosaic in a Romanesque design, and walked through our empty house, ready to fill it with our life, our expectations. Of work. And money. With visits from grown children. With parties… With our vanity.

On moving day, a truck was really not needed, but the movers were required to come with one. It remained parked while our possessions were carried from one side of the street to the other. I had wine and beer and hefty snacks for the movers and everyone else. Moving day was a be-in, and a joyful mess. The very conservative man who had lived next door for ages, whose house was the pride and joy of his life, eventually became very intimidated by his new neighbors. But, on the day of our move, peering from behind his lace curtains at the march of our exposed mélange of eclectic possessions, being hauled from one side of the street to the other, he must have decided that a bunch of hippie crazies were invading his side of the street, just to devalue his property.

"Did you know?" my husband found this out some time after we had become quite settled. "He called a real estate agent to put his house up for sale the very day we moved in."

"That doesn't surprise me," I laughed. "And here he is still."

And here we were. And we were so busy. So-o-o busy. Forcing the solid piece of impulsively acquired, weighty construction of brick and stone and marble to bend to our wills.

We tore and rolled up beige wall-to-wall carpeting. Men with machines came and sanded and polished and restored parquet floors to former splendor on the main floor. With a nasty liquid that required rubber gloves up to my elbow, I stripped the paint from the dining room mantelpiece, uncovering and bringing back the original oak. I buffed and stained the wood with oils and sealers. The walls on the entire main floor were liberated from their grass cloth and the living room was painted in matt, creamy white. The dining room walls we covered with one of my wall papers, inspired by a Kashmir shawl, in lush, sexy undulating swirls of rich, dark reds.

Over our oval, sleek, blond, newly acquired Scandinavian dining room table, Susie's dangling bare light bulb was replaced with our stained glass Tiffany style half globe, we had owned and treasured throughout years of moving to and living in various apartments. We had a recently acquired white linen couch. We bought a wingchair upholstered in a dark blue brocade fabric. And there was that funny old pouf of a swiveling purple velvet chair, my husband liked to sit in when he was writing in his notebook, humming to himself and chewing on the tip of his pencil.

We hung pictures, arranged lamps, put pots and pans and crockery in cupboards. We put our dinner service in the antique armoire we had found at Goodwill and restored. We arranged our drawing desks and art materials, and distributed books on shelves in the third floor studio and in the newly built bookcases in the living room. We had a great time playing with our new giant bauble.

My husband made plans to pull up most of the concrete covering the backyard and start a little garden. We bought a king-sized bed for our luxurious bedroom. We planned to buy,… and we would have,… and we would redo,…and in this corner we would put …, and we would invite ….and Christmas..

Embracing me, mock earnest, my husband said in a stage whisper: "You know, sometime soon we will have to think about getting back to work."

In the master bedroom I was arranging my clothes in the ample dressing alcove closet with a mirror on the door. "Work, work, work." I chanted. "Soon, soon, soon!" I kissed my reflection in the mirror. "Yes, yes, yes!"

3.

Our children were no longer living at home. We were not the foursome we had been. Our son was at music school in Boston. His designated bedroom for the times he came home, was opposite ours facing the back yards. The two adjoining rooms on the top floor were reserved for our daughter. The one with the stuck door during our first house visit was to be her bedroom. The other her studio.

Our daughter had followed a boyfriend with film ambition to LA. A good artist since the first moment she had held a crayon in her little hand, she found work on the backlot at Universal as a scenery and prop builder. She also attended art classes in Pasadena. When she returned after almost two years on the West Coast, minus boyfriend, but with a substantial portfolio of artwork, she moved into her two third floor rooms for a short stay. Not before long she packed up once again, and we drove her to the Yale Drama School to study stage and costume design.

Their leaving, first daughter, then son, had been wrenching. But then, we began to play house and work and life in a new way. This new couple we had become belonged to us. After concentrated hours of work in the mornings in the third floor studio, we often paused in the afternoon, switching gears, spending time with vodka or white wine. While the light in the stained glass windows sprayed rainbow colors on the shiny oak floors in the master bed chamber, we tumbled into the king sized bed, for l'amour l'après midi. I thought we had been "so much older then... we were younger than that now."

For several years to come, the delight of owning the house sustained a permission to take a deep satisfying breath and plunge into what I thought was a graceful, settled, well designed existence. All that unfolded and played and worked and lasted for a time. But the years coming and changing and falling away could not be stopped. I began to sense that life in the house was taking on an insidious murmur of tectonic disjoints. Into the settled ownership of the perfect house, a measured drip-drip of primitive thinking began to seep into my well designed, reasonable, busy existence. My mistrust extended from my coveted house, to all the solid attached surrounding houses hugging, pressing upon each other, holding each other to a mutual contract of orderliness. I began to imagine that something malicious had always been built into the design of these massive 19th century symbols of bourgeois stability.

With windows only in front and back and the long expanse of stonewalls and the weight of the neighboring dwellings on both sides, in spring and summer, with the sun riding higher in the sky and the trees brimming with leaves, the interiors turned darker. All that was explainable. Still I became aware of a vague gloom hovering, in nooks and crannies, never quite letting up or letting go. I felt it lurking around corners, in the walls...waiting at the top or the bottom of the stairs. There was an oppressive something.... a whisper of darkness that had nothing to do with the angle of sunlight not quite penetrating the rooms because of the absence of windows on the side walls, nor the pressure on the walls of our house from the dwellings on each side. The two-family houses across the street also hugged each other tightly on both sides. But they lacked the longer expanse front to back. More light from the windows on the street side and from those facing the backyard was able to filter into rooms in the center.

I began to have wistful moments, during which I had to admit that I missed living in the rented duplex. I missed the large window seat filled with pillows our daughter and I had embroidered. From there, in the mornings, my husband and I, with smiles and trepidations, had watched our girl and her little brother, often holding hands, managing their book bags, traipsing up the street, disappearing around the corner to the neighborhood school.

Our bedroom on the top floor could not compare with the spaciousness and high ceilings of the new master chamber with the king sized bed. The duplex bedroom had doubled as a studio and a television room. It had been the only room with an air conditioner in the window. On sweltering summer nights our children had slept in sleeping bags on the floor. We all watched Nixon's abdication in that all purpose room. From it we stepped onto the roof terrace with plants and patio furniture. High in the air, we used to host summer parties with food and wine and music.

In the dining room and kitchen windows, there had been potted plants dangling from macramé hangings. On the living room wall behind the couch had hung two large, colorful Indian street paintings of Ganesha, the Elephant, and Hanuman, the Monkey.

These folkloric images, given to us by our traveling photographer friend, my husband and I rejected as not quite suitable. We thought our new parlor walls should display a more chic, graphic look. On the creamy, freshly painted walls of our current living room, we arranged small drawings, black and white photographs, and only one large picture of three Victorian women stuffed into coats and furs and oversized hats with veils, my husband had painted in his student days in art school. The Indian paintings were rolled up and stashed away. In front of the semicircular stained glass window our formerly cherished macramé hangings with planters, were replaced with a cluster of tall potted trees in Italian urns.

The roof of the new house had no terrace. We indulged in a fleeting thought of constructing a roof deck. When summer days and heat came, our backyard was useless because of the central air conditioning unit squatting there like a giant toad on the concrete ground. While the roaring, churning machine dispensed chilly comfort into the dark interiors of our fancy house, plans for digging up concrete and planting a garden were postponed and then abandoned.

I did not take me long to admit that the initial triumph of owning an imposing piece of property could not be sustained. It did not take me long to admit that in the more open, more airy duplex, where our life had unfolded in a je ne sais quoi mode, did not follow us across the street to the house. I had to admit that the ownership of status property with its implication of permanence had put me on a march to a slow drumbeat away from younger days into older years. And, I even had to admit, that by moving to the side of the street with greater architectural status, we had relinquished the status view. The view of our impressive Italianate facades belonged to the other, to the lesser side, to Celia's side of the street.

The years had propelled us into our late forties. Our children had been a constant, demanding and rich part of our life. Now they had taken long strides into their futures. From now on I knew that in this house our sweet babes would come "home" only as visitors. My husband and I had not been "older then," becoming "younger than that now."

Our son's bedroom had gradually been transformed into our television viewing room. Yes, his bed was there. And some of his monster movie posters remained on the walls like relics of what had come and gone. An autographed baseball was still displayed on a bookshelf. My husband christened the room "The Menopausal Parlour."

4.

Before our parties my husband and I rehearsed the evening's entertainment with a pianist friend who was always ready to perform his own songs and play for anyone who brought their sheet music. Along with the olio of show tunes and stand-up routines, the dining table groaned under platters laden with an endless variety of buffet dishes I had planned and prepared in the awkward not very large kitchen. And there was always the generous flow of liquor for the ever growing number of the invited.

By the time the actors and professional Manhattan friends and the neighborhood couples were dispersing into cabs and subways or stumbling home on foot, the evening had grown into late night. After these bacchanals, and Christmas parties, stacks of dirty dishes and liquor bottles clogging the kitchen and dining room, I would crawl up the stairs into bed and sink into a dark, stony sleep in our king sized bed and wake in terror and reach for my husband.

"Was I all right?" I would ask in a cobwebby voice, tugging at his pajama.

"Of course you were," he mumbled, "You were great,.. you always are…, my God, … didn't you hear the compliments?"

"All those Manhattan people dragging themselves to Brooklyn," I mumbled. "I have to make it special."

"You really ought to get someone in to help," he said. He often said that.

"No, never!" I was determined not to cave into such things. "This is so god damned suburban! I can't trot out hired help too."

Our parties in the duplex had been no less filled with food and drink and music. But, I remembered them as lighter, easier. During those gatherings I had been less in need to prove myself to be the best ever Park Slope party giver. I was simply asking new and old friends to come to my home for good food and wine and talk and spontaneous burst of singing. In the house, I had begun to endow the parties with an irrational weight and determination of "can you top this!?" The gatherings were becoming a threat to themselves.

Both of us began to drink. A lot. I tried to be careful when I was out in the world. Showing up at an audition or a meeting with an editor with evidence on my breath would not do, but at home I often bounced from pillar to post under the influence most days and every evening.

Owning a house with many rooms meant being in a privileged surrounding of empty rooms. I could only be in any one room at any one time. We worked in the studio on the third floor or sat in "The Menopausal Parlor" watching television. Not much time was spent in the elegant living room with the carefully chosen and placed graphic art on the walls. It had reverted to the status of a Victorian reception salon, only used when someone dropped in.

Or, during those drunken parties.

We rented places by the shore or in Vermont for the summer. We traveled for work and for pleasure. We took trips to Europe. But I became threatened, as I hadn't been before, by the implication that one proved something by having "plans for the week-end." For so long, we had been distanced from conventional routines of work-week and play week-end. With the children gone, their school schedules gone, we had never learned how to breathe life into the meaningless slicing away of the last two days of the week into a separate compartment. Watching the exodus from the street on Friday, watching the Italian family clan next door gathering on Sunday, I should have treasured my liberation from such obligations. I didn't. I was entrapping myself into believing I was being left behind, left out.

The wide street was bordered with huge trees. There they stood, leafy and luxurious in spring and summer, double rows of secretive, whispering sentinels. In autumn the house-proud and tree-proud owners raked city brown leaves in their front and backyards. Bragging about children and schools and summer trips. Leaving for week-ends upstate or New England where the leaves would be red and gold.

"Why are we hanging on to this continuing pretense of being lucky to stay planted in this semi-urban status "palazzo?" I would often sigh.

I started confronting my husband with variations of that question. I thought of our first meeting with Susie. She and her husband had escaped to their jewel of a small house in Manhattan. We had lost touch but heard that they had moved a couple of times. Their latest home was in a new high rise on the Upper East side. I began to long for and project myself into a more anonymous, less neighborly life in a glass tower with urban views on the other side of the East River.

Each time I touched on the subject of leaving the house and the neighborhood, be it lightly or turning it into a wifely nag, I was met with the same unflinching determination:

"I am not going anywhere. We are lucky to be living the way we do." Topping that with a wink he added. "I expect to be carried out of here feet first."

I would pull back. Go back to using the subway rides to learn my lines for the next acting class or the next play or song I was rehearsing.

5.

The apartment in the basement had three rooms. We had not been interested in doing the work the place needed to, maybe, make the place rentable. Not long after we moved in and were concentrating on the redecoration of "our" three floors of the house, in a burst of generosity and grandiosity, we offered the ground floor to our friend from art school. He was the man with the camera, who had to vacate a crumbling tenement dwelling under the elevated on Myrtle Avenue. He subsisted on teaching jobs and grants. He fixed up the basement to his specification. Built a darkroom he could work in. And otherwise created a book filled and livable space to drop into when he returned from India or the hollers of West Virginia or the Haight in San Francisco. We did not charge him rent. When he came back from his journeys with beautiful, ascetic black and white photographs, my husband and I took great pride in our role of his "patrons."

While doing some work on the below stairs apartment, our friend had found a tiny wooden chest with an old letter tucked behind a loose tile in the fireplace. Written in Swedish in 1896, about ten years after the house had been built, it was preserved in good condition and was legible.

"*Kära mamma, pappa ock lilla syster: Jag är förfärligt hemsjuk ock jag längtar på er varje stund. Det är tråkigt at vara ensam. Jag längtar på Sverige. Jag har ingen at språka med. Snart kommer Julen, ock so blir livet ledsnare. Jag kan aldrig gå på kyrkan. Jag hoppas at gode Guden vill färlåta mig ....*"

"*Dear mama and papa and little sister. I miss you all, and I am terribly homesick every moment here. I feel so alone. I have no one to talk to. Christmas will be here soon and that will make life even sadder. I have no chance to go to church. I pray the good Lord will forgive me.*"

The letter had never been sent. For almost ninety years it had stayed in the envelope with a stamp on it.

6.

I was often cast in good parts in small, sometimes satisfying and imaginative, sometimes irritating, downtown theatre productions. When not at work at the drawing desk, there was nothing to keep me on that street, in that house with all those rooms.

My husband did not object to my pursuits. Often praising my performances, he took advantage of the time

I spent away from home. He began to wander off by himself and stay out, late into the night.

Returning from Manhattan from a dance class, a rehearsal, or performance, I would come into an empty house to find notes propped against a vase with flowers on the coffee table. "I got lonely! Stepped out for a while. Love, Me." "Went out for a drink. See you later. Kisses, Me." "I won't be late. Don't be angry!" Always signed with a funny drawing of himself. On the short walk from the subway station, even before I walked up my front steps and put the key in the first door and crossed the Romanesque style mosaic of the little vestibule between the two doors, I began to prepare myself for an evening alone, with only whatever was left in the liquor cabinet to keep me company.

Before me the late evening stretched into night. I listened for the approach of an occasional car or a motorcycle vrooming, coming closer and closer, driving past the house. Before starting to fade away at the turn to the park, the noise of the motor grew explosive, exaggerated.... Even voices from a conversation coming from passersby on the street seemed amplified and grated on me. Every street sound was a reminder that I had allowed myself to become my own willing prisoner within this house. In the bedroom, without the help of daylight streaming through the stained glass, no rainbows danced on the floor. The windows turned blind. Alone inside my vodka haze, waiting, the walls of the house at night were even more oppressive than during daylight. I would doze hoping to hear the key in the front door followed by the sound of my husband's footsteps on the stairs.

One night he was especially late coming back. I gave up on pretending to be untouched by what I no longer could deny to myself. Ashamed to be lying there in the king sized marriage bed, drunk and exhausted, not knowing what to think or do anymore, I went up to the third floor, to the room that Susie had avoided opening, the morning we had first looked at the house. Since our daughter was rarely in need of that room, it had been turned into a guest room. On the platform bed with a futon, I fell into a drunken sleep. I was wakened by a violent shaking of the bed. I sat up. No lights were on.

"Is that you?" I cried, expecting to see my husband. No one was there.

Some time after we had moved from across the street, we had learned from Celia, the neighborhood chronicler, that the wife of the couple who had owned the house before Jay and Susie, had a child who died in one of the twin bedrooms on the third floor. My daughter didn't know any of this. Still, she had avoided sleeping in her designated bedroom. When she was home she slept on the couch in the living room. Or on a cot in the adjoining room, her studio.

Was there really a darkness in this house? Lurking within the corners and within the walls gradually seeping out and injecting poison into the life of its inhabitants even before us? And now continuing to poison the life of two people who had trusted in their love and affection for each other and for their children, and taken pleasure in their work and good life?

During the worse moments of facing the regrets, the crumbling of that life, and, yes, shame staring me in the face, I began to cave into remnants of beliefs from a long, long ago time. I was being punished for something. For arrogance, for taking for granted the exceptional permanence of my solid marriage, for having become too prideful or too ignorant to face an oncoming crash. Being the proprietor of a piece of fancy property compensated for refugee days, displacement, sweltering summers in New York City. It was in this house that I had to look into the heart of what I should have known. It was in this house, I had to bow down and accept, that I myself had chosen to ignore signal flags that had been fluttering in my direction for quite some time.

Could Celia have been the unwitting messenger at a crossroads? She had come to us and pointed us in the direction of temptation. We had crossed the street with fear and trembling and glee in our hearts and souls. In our destined house we had looked up at the ceilings, we had looked down at the floors, we had looked at each other.

"Yes," we had said: "Yes. We like this," we had said. "Yes, we want it. Yes, we had said. "We should,… we must have it. Yes."

On another night, drunk, out of my mind, I turned on the water in the bathtub on the second floor. I forgot it and passed out in the bedroom. I woke up from a stupor late the next day. The water had cascaded through the inner wall down to the basement apartment. The luscious crimson wallpaper in the dining room appeared to have survived. But, as the walls stayed moist and did not dry, the paper began to detach itself and crawl and crinkle. Our photographer friend in the basement apartment had a substantial collection of books. Many were damaged.

As our marriage unraveled, the close friend became distant, hiding in his darkroom and behind his subsidized independence in the basement. I had latched on to this friendship, which, in art school had belonged to my husband alone. Somewhere along the way, I had to face the fact that my husband's devotion to the admired photographer had not always been strictly platonic.

"Get rid of him!" I would scream in my most shrewish moments. "He takes advantage of us in his rent-free lair below stairs! He is just a moocher"!

"You are making him into a scapegoat," my husband came back with lame excuses. "Blaming him for our instabilities."

Yes, he was right. Passing the blame was pointless. My problems, our problems were much bigger than peeling wallpaper and the waterlogged books of an aloof, shrinking away friend, in the basement.

One evening, when I had been left alone once again, I rooted around in the underwear drawer of my husband's dresser. Looking for I didn't know what. Well, I found it! Wrapped in a sock, I found a packet of condoms and a jar of Vaseline. How much longer should I allow myself to be made a fool of? Believing that he was stepping out for a drink or two, to sit on a barstool in some bar on Christopher Street to have a convivial chat about the talent of Bette Midler, or the merit or lack of it in the latest Broadway musical? I could imagine the psychobabble crowds, led by Celia, pointing fingers, shaking heads and whispering about me:

"That poor woman is in total denial."

That night he came home even later than usual, more drunk than usual, I was not drunk. I chased him down the stairs hurling a pair of scissors at his head, dislodging his glasses, barely missing his right eye. I pulled a small picture off the wall and got ready to slam it down on his head. I changed my mind and threw it at a standing lamp. The picture was destroyed. The lamp was in pieces. There was glass scattered everywhere. I sat down on the bottom step. He sank into his purple chair. With backs turned to each other, both of us began to cry.

After a moment had passed my husband stood up and said, "I'll sweep up the broken glass."

I climbed up the stairs to the bedroom and crept into that huge bed. I could hear the swish of a broom, guiding shards onto a dustpan. He was fastidious. We often walked around the house barefoot. I heard the pieces of glass fall into the trashcan in the kitchen. I held my breath. Would he come to bed? I wanted him to. I wanted everything bad to be swept away, erased. Like pictures that had been worked on and coaxed onto the page at night, and had to be abandoned on the drawing desk, to be rethought, and redrawn in the light of day.

At last, I heard his footsteps on the stairs. He did not turn on any lights when he came into the bedroom. He moved around to the other side of the bed. I listened to him undress, fold his clothes and lay them on a nearby chair. He pulled his pajamas from under the pillows and put them on. First the pants, then the top. He climbed into bed and hovered at the edge as far away from me as he could. I was rigid, clutching my side of the mattress. The space between us was large enough for the effigy of our dying marriage. When I heard his regular breath turn into quiet snores, I got up and went back downstairs.

I sat on the couch and tried to imagine a scene: I pack a bag. I walk out to the vestibule and close the first door. I walk through the second door, making sure it does not bang when it shuts behind me. I descend the stone steps to the street. And continue walking. I turn the corner by the park and walk to the subway stop on Grand Army Plaza. I can see it all as if I were following a tracking shot in a film.

Exhausted, frightened, I curled up among the soft throw pillows on the couch and fell asleep.

I woke up to the smell of coffee and the sound of breakfast dishes clattering in the kitchen. I got up and stepped outside into a fine, sunny spring morning, reassured by The Times waiting to be picked up on the front steps of our house. My husband was sitting at the dining room table with his cup of coffee before him. He got up and came back from the kitchen with a large mug of coffee with milk and a slice of already buttered toast which he put in front of me. We didn't mention the night before. We divided sections of the paper between us.

Time passed. We went on as before. Out of fear of change. Out of shame.

In the end, when back tracking, compromising, accepting, half forgiving, could no longer be held on to, he was the one who delivered the ultimate coup-de-grace.

7.

He had been late that afternoon picking me up at La Guardia. When, at last, I saw him walking toward me at the baggage claim, my first thought was to ask, "Why are you so late?" But I stopped myself. I was happy to be back on the ground after a bumpy flight from Rochester, where I had spent two nights shooting a commercial in a big local Italian market after hours. One night, I had gushed and praised, in Italian, the freshness of vegetables and fruit in the produce area. The next night I did the same for the dairy and cheeses. The commercial was shot MOS, an old Hollywood expression adapted from the German meaning "without sound." We could not fake what we were saying because the phrases had to be authentic for lip readers. Until the director was pleased, there were many takes. It was a local but big commercial. It paid well up front.

After the shoot wrapped, I had returned to the hotel to find the red light blinking on the phone in my room. I picked up the short and sweet recorded message: "I love you." That was all. I wanted to call my husband back, but it was past 2:00 AM. I hadn't wanted to spoil the thought by waking him late at night. I fell asleep exhausted, happy, ready to go home.

At the La Guardia parking lot, I tossed my bag in the back seat. He maneuvered our Volvo onto the afternoon traffic on the Long Island Expressway. All through the ride back to Brooklyn I chattered about the shoot. The mishaps, The retakes, ... It wasn't until we were home and he had gone upstairs with my bag that I remembered that I had ignored how silent he had been during the entire ride from the airport. When I said, "Your message last night was so sweet! Thank you!" he had only managed a pinched smirk. He was concentrating on the driving, of course. The traffic was awful.

Between the leafy tall plants the early evening light of May, filtered through the semicircular stained glass window into the penumbra of the living room. I had flopped onto the couch and kicked off my shoes. My feet always swelled on airplane flights. I had closed my eyes. I was sweating. I had been wearing the same dress since early morning. I was longing for a shower and thinking about the neighborhood Italian restaurant we often went to for a quick dinner. After taking my bag upstairs to the bedroom, he came hurrying back down the stairs. Planted two steps in front of me stood the rigid figure of a man. With a scowl on his face and hands stuck into the pockets of his jeans, stared and me and said:

"I have moved out. I have left you."

"What are you talking about?" I said, as if I were really asking a question. Trying a laugh, I added, "Your timing is splendid!"

His eyes behind the glasses had become nasty slits. His face looked oily and gray.

"I AM A HO-MO-SEX-UAL!" he came back at me, spelling the word syllable by syllable. He began to pace. "You know it. I know it."

He began pacing. Then sank into the blue brocade armchair. It was then I noticed that his swiveling purple chair was gone.

"Don't you see!" his voice in support of his announcement, growing into a shout,

"Don't you see, that you and I have been in a toxic relationship for too long…"

"You sound idiotic!" I won't start screaming, I promised myself. I won't hit him. I did manage another deep laugh. My God!.... Toxic relationship! Who had whispered that bit of recent self help, psychobabble lingo in his ear?

"Who provided you with this crutch to help you limp away?"

To that he had nothing to say.

"Now, what am I to do exactly?" I heard myself say. To the room, to our life, to the plants…. "And, why did you leave me that message last night?"

"Damn it, I do love you." The trite, hackneyed phrase hung in the air between us. "I just can't live with you anymore. I do love you," he repeated. "Or I would have left a long time ago."

I had to take a deep breath before I could counter him.

"No, you wouldn't have." I let my voice drop down into a deep, low region in my gut. "No, you would NOT have," I said. "NOT before Stonewall. NOT before official Gay Pride marches. NOT before all the noise and rainbow flag waving and self righteous declarations and demands for rights. You wouldn't have had the guts to crawl out from your protective wife-and-children shelter."

"You forget Matthew," he said. "I would not have done it without Matthew coming into my life."

Matthew! That little kraut from the Rhineland! With his treble voice, his fawning and his mincing and his nowhere singing career. In a long ago century he would have been a castrato. Yes, he had been around. Another nice friend with aspirations to performing. There was a cluster of those in our lives. We were the glamour couple. We shared interest in music and theatre. No different than the other gay theatrical and artist friends in my, in both our circle. Crowding our parties.

Matthew had been the one who had tipped the scale? He was the one-and-only who had given my husband courage to give himself permission to get away from me?

All this, after we had climbed out of complete poverty level student lives, produced fine offspring, and shared much joy and work together. Solid things. Everybody had problems. It was worth overlooking sexual proclivities, ridiculous marital confrontations... In the end nothing should lead to the destruction of the validity of this domestic scene, this marriage. In it I had done my share, had played my part vigorously and well. I had cooked good meals and baked bread and made him and my children clothes. On the top floor of this house, as in all the more modest places we had occupied, we had sat side by side at our desks, drawing and painting little clever and charming pictures that had led to appreciation and to money. We had collected memories of Christmas and photographs of happy moments and phone calls that brought good news. All that was being bulldozed and wrecked because of Matthew?!

We had both been so young. Good, cozy lover friends, taken by surprise, delighted to have found each other. He had been timid about many things, both in and out of bed. I had always accepted a certain pudeur in his lovemaking. Making allowances and brushing aside far away ideas of what I sometimes allowed myself to think I might be missing. If he was a little reticent in bed it was because he wasn't a brute. He was sweet and sensitive. He was an artist. He was my husband. I was his wife. We had concentrated on the pretty babies we had made, but, as they grew into often tiresome and demanding teenagers, the constant focus on the children had loosened its grip. The girl and boy had arrived on the cusp of becoming fine world weary, intelligent adults. Artists in their own right.

During our wine infused afternoons of lovemaking, I had noticed a change in him. He aroused me with newer, with subtler skills. In ways that surprised and excited me. Those afternoons he was turning me, his longtime wife into a concubine. Not wanting to complete the suspicious thoughts about how and if he may have acquired new skills outside of our marriage bed, I persuaded myself that being by ourselves for ourselves, our lovemaking had been liberated. We could reclaim and reshape the younger us we hadn't had time for in our early life together.

"Please don't go," I said very quietly. "Don't leave. I don't care what you do. It really is not important…Don't leave me….."

"You poor woman!" he shouted. "What have I done to you? You must not like sex…! There are things men do to women I have never done to you!"

I felt as if my innards were being scraped out with a trowel. Leaving a hollow cavity where my life had been stored until this late afternoon. I was sitting, frozen and still on the couch in the living room decorated just so in our restrained graphic style. I felt a rancid odor wafting out of my mouth, from my pores, from out of my female body. Light streaming through the semicircular stained glass window would last for yet another hour or so, before the sun disappeared.

And then, as if he were a judge passing a generous and unexpected decree, the pompous, newly awakened hedonist declared;

"Don't you see that I am giving you your freedom!"

I looked around at the floor to ceiling bookcases. So many books had been gifts. For birthdays. For Mother's Day. For Christmas. A book of paintings by Pietro Longhi, the chronicler, who painted witty genre scenes of 18th century well-to-do domesticated Venetians, had been a present after our last trip to Venice. He had inscribed it, "Kisses to my amore, that's the long and the short of it." In a French book about Marie Antoinette, he had written, "To the one who has always allowed me to eat cake."

"When I was in bed pregnant and nauseous," I blurted out. "You used to read to me….. what are we to do with all the books?"

"What's the big deal?" he said. "You'll take yours, I'll take mine."

"I thought they were our books," I said

"I am leaving you the house," he said jumping up from the wing chair.

"I have to go now," he added. "Matthew will be waiting with supper."

He thought he was taking a leap into a new adventure. He wasn't. He was sneaking away from one domesticated life and burrowing into another. Matthew was waiting with supper! Wrapped in a lacy apron no doubt. Setting the table for two with Bavarian china. Vocalizing. My husband was not taking a leap into freedom. He was merely making a move into another set of four walls with bedroom and bathroom and kitchen and dining table ....and supper!

Had he temper-tantrummed himself into this Matthew nonsense...? Was he trying to toss our life into a dirty burlap sack to hurl it down his new road of liberation? Or maybe only down the front steps of this house.....,? Was he dragging me into the eruption of an trumped up war ...? No, he was having a temper tantrum! That's was all,,,! A temper tantrum... That's what it was... Not war. This could all rewind, be set to right....We had done it before. Upstairs to bed we would go,... And, in the morning there would be fresh coffee and toast and the Times on the breakfast table....

He tossed a folded piece of paper onto the coffee table. "Here is our phone number."

"May I venture to ask if "our" phone is located in a place with an address?"

"Matthew said not to let you have it," was the pathetic response. "He is afraid you will murder us."

Something snapped in me there and then.

"How flattering!" I managed to balance a witchy laugh on a snarl. I might yet find a way to do the deed. And fly away on Medea's fiery getaway chariot.

"Talk to a divorce lawyer," he said. "I already have."

Other people talked to divorce lawyers. Other people got trapped in houses they no longer wanted.

Other people...... I thought I had evaded being one of those other people.

"Get out!" I hissed at him. "And, hurry," I added. "You don't want your supper to get cold!"

I hated myself. For not tearing his glasses off his face and stomping on them. For not grabbing a sharp object and gouging out his cute little eyes. For not helping my exiting husband a decisive kick in the balls.

On his way out of the house, he didn't slam the first door to the vestibule with the tiled floor. He didn't slam the outside door. I listened for his footsteps going down the stone steps, continuing down the street, fading, until I could hear them no longer after he turned left toward the subway station on Grand Army Plaza.

He was "giving me my freedom!" So that I would find real, good sex I had never known with men, who "did things" to women. He was leaving me the house! This was a double dose of pure malice. I was the one who wanted to get out of this house. Away from the whole self satisfied populace of the neighborhood. He was the one who had not wanted to budge.

How could I have tied myself into knots all those late nights, when his absence gave me license to head in the direction of the liquor bottles on their special shelf in the polished wood cabinet. All those times he had equated my rushing to rehearsals or dance classes with his; "I got lonesome-stepped out for a drink." What layers of cobwebs had I not been able to wipe aside? He wasn't lying. He simply wasn't spelling things out in skywriting.

The man had ambushed me! He had made me filthy. I had allowed him to make me filthy. I had clung to my blindness because of his wit and sweetness. And a genuine admiration for his talent and growing success. How long would it take me to pull myself up and out of the sludge I had been wading in? Before I began my quest for great sex with real men.

His newfound arrogant posturing may have sustained my fury the immediate moments following his exit. When the first flush began to fade, I had to face the dread of spending the night in the house alone. "Alone" in a brand new way. I was too exhausted and drained to call a friend, to leave and go in search of somewhere to crash. Or search for a shoulder. Not to cry on, no. More likely to regurgitate justifications and hurts.

"What does that fawning nonentity have," I cried a few days later to one of my gay actor friends, "That I don't?!"

"Darling, don't be daft," came the blunt response from the horse's mouth. "Matthew does have something you don't. He has a dick."

As simple as that. As banal as that. As obvious as that.

My husband had broken me. He had. Even worse than his breaking me, I had allowed him to turn me into a stupid woman. Stupid for having looked away, pushed aside as unimportant what had been staring me in the face for a long time. To have been so full of fear, so desperate to hide my shameful knowing. Then moments before he left I had become a desperate beggar, further erasing myself, with my pleading: "Don't go,...I don't care what you do!" Heaping still more shame on myself by clinging to a man, who no longer wanted me. Who had not wanted me for a long time, maybe never. I was blaming myself not only for not having burst out of a cocoon of faux security, but for staying in a union I was arrogant enough to have trusted to be better, stronger, unlike the one next door, or down the street, or the next block. Because within the edifice of our marriage, built of unshakable comradeship and romance, I had convinced myself that his homosexuality was no more than an allergy I could overlook and accept!

8.

The next task was to take the first, then the second and third step, into tonight, into the next morning and the next afternoon. And the coming clusters of days and weeks stretching before me. The phone calls I would have to make. To confess that my solid, perfect marital union had crashed. To admit that I had joined the crowd I had never wanted to belong to.

"Yes, it became unavoidable." "No, I'll tell you more soon." "Thank you, I'll be...I am alright."

But, for heaven's sake, for right now, for this moment, get out of this sweat soaked dress that feels as if it had fused to my skin. Go upstairs and take a shower!

After he was gone I spent a long time letting hot and cold water pour over me in the shower; my night lasted a lifetime of thrashing in that fouled king sized bed. Between dozing and waking I groped for his pajama that wasn't there. I couldn't shake the habit of listening for the sound of his key turning in the lock of the front door. In the morning malicious rays of sunlight filtered through the stained glass in the windows. I thought of the morning my husband and I had first looked at the house. When in this bedroom Susie told her little three year old daughter of "dancing rainbows," on the floor. The girl was in high school now.

It wasn't only the nights that were to be awful since he had gone. The days stretched before me. I couldn't eat. I couldn't think of going up to the top floor with only one drawing desk where two had nestled side by side. The studio even more than the bedroom was a reminder of desecration.

I remember seeing a primitive Mexican painting of a saint at the stake. Naively rendered flames, not unlike an image in a comic strip were erupting all over his tortured body, while the martyr's twisted, agonized mouth pleaded to heaven for release. I felt as if hot little flames were erupting from my hair, from my breasts from my thighs. But, just as the martyrs had done through the ages, I had invited humiliation and hurt. Long years of the day-to-day maneuvers and solutions of domestic problems, the hopeful making of plans, discussions of the next purchase to enhance the household, the next vacation trip, the next pleasing and educating of children, were falling away like the charred flesh of a determined but misguided saint.

I had been dragged out of Mass that freezing Christmas morning in Kraków in 1944 by the Nazis barging into the chapel, booting everyone at gunpoint into the courtyard of the Benedictine convent where I had been sheltered, along with a few remaining Jews hiding in plain sight. They made us line up with our backs to them facing the brick wall that surrounded the convent. I had on a flimsy skirt and a worn thin sweater. My coat had been left behind in the chapel pew. One of the Nazi's shoved me so close to the wall, I felt my nose scraping against the icy red brick. I felt the butt of his rifle right behind my right ear. I stood there, lined up with the other Juden, waiting for the shot. I was not frightened. No. I had become one with the icy air around me, trying to hold on to the thought that would be the last in my almost ten year old brain: When he shoots, I wondered, will there be a split second of time for me to form a memory of the hole the bullet will make when it pierces my scull? Then I felt the rifle slide away. The Nazi did not waste his bullet on me. It was then I began to freeze and shake.

And now, my husband of almost thirty years had abdicated his bed and walked out closing the door to our house, to our life, to "go home" to one of the offspring of the master race. Who was keeping his supper warm! If I hadn't been so destroyed and spent, I could, I should have allowed myself to look straight into the black humor of the cosmic joke played on me. My husband was tearing me out of his life, out of our life together. He was declaring that he was "giving me my freedom. His gift of "freedom" was making me cave into the shame of an outcast, a reject once again.

I had some fine small pieces of antique jewelry he had given me over the years. Pearls, an Art Nouveau broach, a delicate diamond pendant on a chain, diamond earrings... All lovingly presented on a birthday, or an anniversary. Or Christmas. I kept the pieces wrapped in velvet pouches with drawstring closings in a small jewelry box. It fit easily into a large handbag I now kept with me at all times. I began to go to the bank every day to check if I was still part of a joint account. I withdrew a large sum of cash that I carried around in my handbag along with the jewelry. I had no idea what money would stay mine at this point.

I was trying to envision a time in two years or six months or maybe in thirty one days, when I would see these two guys together, their romance and lust all used up, in domestic arguments about whose turn it was to make the bed in the morning or wash the dishes at night.

9.

One night, on the bed in what had been my son's room, which had become "the menopausal parlor," I fell asleep before the flickering light from the television screen, watching Charles Laughton as Henry VIII doing away with several wives.

I was in a large room lit with candlelight glow from crystal chandeliers. Everything was the way it was meant to be set up for a banquet. Except that the guests at the round tables looked as if they had been smeared and smudged into being with quick, rough brushstrokes or fingers. My husband and I were alone at our table. We were not talking to each other. I turned toward the man sitting behind me at the next table and began to talk to him. I pointed out a woman at a table a little ahead of us. She was not roughly painted or smudged. She seemed to have been rendered in a delicate line with a fine pen point. She was very beautiful and animated and talking to herself.

    "Oh, yes, that is the famous Madame X," said Mikhail Baryshnikov. " How I wish you would introduce me to her."

    "I'll see if I can catch her attention," I said.
I wanted to be of help to Misha. But I couldn't tell him that I had no idea who the woman was.

    When I looked back in the direction of the beautiful Madame X, she was changed. She had become disheveled. Oil and butter seemed to have been rubbed into her face and hair. Long thin strands of it, limp and greasy, were covering her face. She was gesturing and babbling incoherent half words and syllables. Blue saliva trickled out of both corners of her mouth. At her table, she was surrounded by seven men with their arms entwined around each other. They were dressed in black choir robes with faces hidden behind black Commedia masques with protruding beaklike noses. They rocked to-and-fro and began to sing, "We shall overco-o-o-ome," over and over again, changing keys and harmonies. Then their song changed to "Freude Schöne Götterfunkel" I heard no orchestra. Not even a piano accompaniment.

    "Why isn't the dance band playing?" I asked Baryshnikov. Trying to divert his attention from the

messy Madame X. Not only because I couldn't and didn't want to introduce him to her, but because I wanted to discuss with him the hot dogs wrapped in brioche rolls on the paper plates set before us.

"Why is there no Honey Dijon Mustard," I was about to ask Misha. He was not there anymore. I turned back to my husband. He was gone too.

I was no longer alone. Three fat men, their faces pink and puffy, dressed in tuxedo jackets and bow ties, had arrived at my table. They wore knee length little boy pants, and no shirts. On their feet they wore black patent leather loafers. Their black silk socks had unsnapped from knee garters and rolled down around their ankles.

Stepping on feet right and left, I pushed through the trio, asking, "Have you seen him?"

A dance band did begin to play "The Tennessee Waltz." Baryshnikov on point was partnering a man in a red leotard. The man danced well with Misha but he had ugly teeth protruding over his lower lip. His jaw, unshaven huge and lumpy, looked as if an extra large Idaho baking potato had been grafted onto his face. A sound of clapping hands erupted from the tables.

I spotted my husband half reclining in a window seat. Behind him I could see a semicircular window, inset with pieces of stained glass, scintillating with brilliant colors. He was whispering to someone. When he saw me, he put two fingers to his lips. A small man jumped up from behind the plants. Before he gimped away into the perspective of a corridor lined with medieval arches, I recognized Charles Laughton.

"Are you doing this again?" I cried, hitting my husband with my fists. "Are you?"

My husband's eyes had become narrow slits. His face was smudging and fading away.

"Who is it this time?" I hissed. "Quasimodo?"

"I met him in the park," my husband giggled.

"I am kicking you out," I said.

All at once, neat geometric designs in red lines and squares, like the kind kitchen towels are often patterned in, began to cover his face and neck.

"Wipe those things off your face!" I knew I was supposed to be screaming, "You can't hide from me anymore!" No sounds were coming out of my throat. My thoughts were staying somewhere deep inside, behind silent vocal chords!

Gasping for breath, I followed a zig-zag pattern in the parquet floor toward a French window opening onto a garden. A small yellow airplane had crashed from the sky into a grove of fir trees. I ran toward the flames and woke up.

Charles Laughton had taken his Henry VIII with him and left the television screen.

I was shaken by the vivid dream. It must have lasted only a few moments. But, when I looked at my watch, it told me I had slept for several hours. Somehow, for the first time in a long time, I woke to a morning I thought might grow into a promising day.

I looked around the walls of my son's room. A room in which he was only a visitor now. Several of his cherished monster movie posters were staring at me from the walls. There was "The Hunchback" and the "Wolf Man" and "Dracula," his favorite.

There hung a photograph of himself at sixteen, dressed for Halloween, plastic fangs protruding from his vampire grin, he had on a black cape with pointed collar, lined in blood red silk. I had sewed it for him and included an embroidered label "Made with love by Mama."

After an endless stream of dark nights of the soul, I made a decision to begin the rise out from under the moping and chewing on myself. Not on your life would I sit here immured in this cursed ton of bricks, on this manicured street turning into the woman in the attic of 19th Century literature.

I knew what I had to do. And fast. It had taken us an hour to decide to buy the house. I would move with equal speed to unload it. I called the only real estate broker I knew from social events in the neighborhood. I had never liked this very composed, bony woman with the tightly cropped hair and well bred voice. I made no secret of the reason for selling. "I am sorry, so sorry," she drawled. I had no wish to take her on a room-to-room tour. The house was pristine, slumbering, in a coma, dead. I told the broker I'd drop off a set of keys. "Feel free to take a look at your convenience," I said.

I dialed the phone number I had on the piece of scrap paper he had tossed on the coffee table the night he walked out.

"I have called the broker," without preamble I told him, "I am putting the house up for sale.

"Why do you have to be in such a hurry," he said, sounding rattled, sheepish. I heard vocalizing and hung up on him.

REAL ESTATE

1.

She divorce lawyer was seated across a massive desk. Behind a huge window a cyclorama of cobalt blue was embracing the New York City skyline. The lawyer facing me was a handsome, slim woman wearing an impeccable white silk blouse, tight fitting plaid skirt and several very thin gold bracelets dangling on her right wrist. On the left, she had a status watch, probably a Rolex. Her blond hair was twisted into one of those tight coils, making me think of one of Hitchcock's cool blonds. I was wearing jeans, a tee shirt and sandals. I was asked to "please, have a seat."

Across the desk stacked with document folders and a yellow pad or two, and a new word processor, I sank into the deep and comfortable leather chair, clutching my handbag with all the pouches of jewelry. During the war, my mother had managed to save some of her jewelry from being taken by the Nazis, by sewing it into seams of her clothing. I imagined that in the interior of the law office, facing the well put together attorney, I must have presented the appearance of a street person cradling a plastic bag.

I dove right into those disgusts and disappointments, festering since that late afternoon, my husband walked out of our house of our life. Then, I launched into a long list of the nice things and happy times and the many ways he had been loving and sweet and funny and had been for years. And what a wonderful father he had always been to our children.

"These things happen," the lawyer sighed. Her voice dripping professional sympathy. "That's why I am here."

"I don't know why I am here," I said. "I don't expect to be haggling about money and possessions."

"For all of his bravado," the lawyer went on, "right now, he must be feeling shaken and guilty. But can you trust the little voice by his side that will, no doubt, be whispering in his ear?"

Actually, I had touched on, but not yet completed, that thought. I said nothing. I nodded in agreement. Other people went to divorce lawyers. Other people allowed their lives to crumble. Other people thought of revenge. I was sitting in an expensive, designer office chair, clutching to my chest my handbag packed with the loving gifts of jewelry from my husband of many years and money we had earned together. I was counseled to follow an alien protocol from somewhere out there, by a woman who perched smartly on the spoils of crumbling couples.

The smooth lawyer picked up one of the yellow pads and a pen, assuring me that she was on my side, ready to look out for my interests.

"First we have to have a separation agreement," she said. "We must have it in writing."

As soon as I left the office with a folder of papers to sign, I found a payphone and called my husband to let him know that I had engaged a lawyer.

That he was legally responsible for paying her fees. That our house was about to sell for a good amount of money. That I thought, when it did, we should split the take right down the middle. That he had to help me look for an apartment in Manhattan right away.

    Only a couple of days after my meeting with the divorce lawyer, I was surprised by a phone call from a broker in another local real estate office. I didn't know her. She had always admired the house from the street, she told me. I didn't ask how or from whom she had heard about the house sale. There were many Celias in the neighborhood. I was sure tongues laced with schadenfreude were wagging.

    "I love the Italian façade," the broker gushed into my ear. My first impulse was to blow her off. Something made me change my mind. She didn't know me or my husband. I was just a woman with a property for sale.

    "If you want to come right over," I said," I have a little time to show you around." I had a lot of time. Within twenty minutes, the new real estate agent was ringing the doorbell.

    Emily was friendly, a little shapeless in a long flower printed skirt and roomy pink cotton sweater, wearing sensible flats. Her hair was mousy brown, pulled back into a short ponytail. At once, I felt at ease with this woman. She made me think of the many teachers and librarians my husband and I were used to meeting at children's book conferences.

    Climbing stairs, going from room to room with the unthreatening broker, the sense of capitulation and defeat and shame that had been choking me since my husband closed the door behind him, loosened. I began to feel as if I were in a play acting the part of a woman who was selling an old house.

The broker bent down to look at a little framed picture that hung at almost floor level on a wall in the narrow hallway between the dining room and the kitchen. "How cute!" she said.

It was one of my husband's pictures of an anthropomorphic cat.

With wrinkled brow and anxious whiskers, the cat, dressed in a proper suit with a napkin knotted around his neck, sits at a table clutching a knife and fork. Behind him the hands on the face of a grandfather clock suggest dinner hour. The plate in front of the cat is empty.

"Our cat died not long ago," I said. "This was his "dining room."

"I left his picture in place, as an altar in his honor.

"I have a new cat," Emily said. "When my other cat died, it took me a long time before I got my new one."

I liked Emily. I just knew I was doing something right by taking her on this polite house tour. I had a feeling that she could make the cursed place be gone. And fast.

But, until she mentioned the considerably higher asking price than the first broker had quoted, I had not thought of my husband's and my home as "real estate." As soon as Emily left with a handshake and smiles and my promise that keys would be delivered un, deux, trois, to her office, I called the chilly, more renown seller of

Park Slope homes to tell her I had decided to go with another agent to handle the sale.

A momentary crack appeared in the mellifluous timbre of the voice of the first lady of Park Slope real estate. She let me know that she was not happy with my decision. I let her know that I was not so very happy at the moment myself.

There was something about the demeanor of this woman, married to a real estate developer of local note, which unearthed memories of the confused, newly arrived me I had been in New York City. Before well turned phrases in English flowed easily from my brain into my mouth. Before I had acquired a proper husband and beautiful children and marketable skills. Before I had a dinner service of fine china displayed behind glass in the dining room breakfront. Before I had scintillating inserts of stained glass in living room and bedroom windows. And, air conditioning. I imagined my slick real estate lady had lived among such things while she was growing up in her parents' house. Before she was sent off to the expected proper finishing school somewhere on the Eastern Seaboard. Where, most likely, she would have been "finished" with a degree in art history.

"Please, return my keys as soon as possible," I said.

The house sold quickly. Emily listed it for a price five times that we had paid. And got it. The unexpected surprise of the money brought me a bit of solace. I tried to put a lid on the ruminating of my disgrace and my shame. A time of something not yet known, not yet making demands, maybe something promising was waiting, over there, on the other side of the river.

On the morning of the contract signing, the woman who was buying the house did not show up in the lawyer's office. She had called to say that her astrological chart forbade her to sign any important papers on that day. A perfect buyer for this house, I thought. Maybe I should have consulted an astrology chart before our impulsive, "This is beautiful, we will take it," decision, more than eleven years before.

A week later the stars had aligned perfectly for the buyer. She signed her name on the designated line.
I had been out of the house, out of Park Slope, out of Brooklyn for a few months when I found out from the lawyer who had done the closing that the house buyer, new owner of the elegant property, on the perfect street near the beautiful park, turned out to be very allergic to cats.

Before broom sweeping ourselves out of the door we had the place thoroughly and professionally cleaned. But the dander our poor little cat had left behind resisted professional vacuum cleaners and strong antiseptic fluids that hovered in crevices and corners. Maybe the buyer ought to have trusted the initial misaligning of the stars, I thought. How long would it take for vapors, other than cat dander, to begin wafting out of the walls.

Several months after the closing I was taking vigorous steps into my new life in my new space in Soho, I was surprised by a phone call and invitation to lunch.

It was then that the lawyer, who had feared my "unlucky" house grumbling might have sabotaged the easy sale, expanded on the version of Celia's tale of what had taken place in the third floor bedroom when the house had belonged to the couple from whom Susie and Jay had bought the house.

They were a handsome successful, childless couple. He a dentist. She an editor in a small literary publishing house. Before the wife at the age of 43 gave birth to a beautiful little baby boy his mother and father, had been mainly focused on their work. With the arrival of their little son, their attention became entirely absorbed in their child.

Then, a late December afternoon just before Christmas, seen by a few neighbors, a small bundle was carried out on a stretcher to a waiting ambulette. The little boy, not yet six months old, had contracted some kind of lethal infection that attacked his lungs. In a few days he was brought home from the hospital. He lingered for a while. But, nothing could be done. He died in his bedroom on the third floor.

The couple picked up and moved away. Real estate agents and lawyers were in charge of the sale of the house. Movers came, emptied it out, making way for the new owners, Susie and Jay. No one in the neighbor hood ever heard anything about them again.

I remembered my husband's and my first walk through and Susie's flimsy explanation about the stuck door to the twin room on the third floor. And then my daughter not wanting to use the room to sleep in. And, at last, one of my dark nights of the soul and the shaking mattress.

"Why didn't Susie and Jay ever tell us about the dead baby," I said.

"Why would they have wanted to spook you," said the lawyer. "And sabotaged their easy sale."

"Nothing would have stopped us," I sighed. "All that 'spook' stuff came later."

And the lawyer had more to tell. In the local pages of the New York Times, he had recognized the couple in a news story tucked away at the back of the paper.

"TOMORROW AND TOMORROW......"

1.

The man had fixed himself a drink, lit a cigarette and settled into the ample wing chair in the living room of their apartment on a high floor in a new building in Chelsea. From a corner window one could catch the view of the Hudson River. Except for some light filtering from the street below and the reading lamp on the side table next to him, the room was dark. She came out of the bedroom and walked past him. At the middle window facing the street, she reached for the hem of her knee length nightdress, pulled it over her head and tossed it on the floor. Then she hoisted herself onto the windowsill and put her left leg through the opened window.

He jumped out of the chair, not knowing, in that moment, what to do with his cigarette, he dropped it into the unfinished drink. The glass slipped from his hand and rolled on the floor.

"It didn't break?" he mused.

He grabbed hold of her and half dragged, half carried her toward the couch. She moaned a little, but didn't resist him. Her eyes were closed. He left her and went to pick up the nightdress and held it out to her. At first she didn't make a move. Then, as if she had been taken by surprise to find herself half reclining on her living room sofa with nothing on, she stood up and reached out her arms toward him, took the garment he was holding up in front of her, and lifted it over her head..

He looked at the tangled, unkempt mass of grey streaked auburn hair that seemed not to have been combed or brushed for days. He watched her slip the nightgown over her body with the little breasts and still flat, well shaped midsection with the delicate "inny" navel and fall below the triangle of thinning hair, until it reached to just above his wife's knees.

"I don't know how much longer I can take this," he mumbled to himself.

Without a word or a look in his direction she rose from the couch and walked toward the bedroom. There followed the sound of running water in the bathroom sink. A reassuring, ordinary sound of preparations for night. Then he listened for her almost inaudible steps moving toward the bed.

He stood in the doorway to the bedroom and watched her climb on top of the bedspread. She lay down on her back, straight and rigid as an effigy, folding her arms across her chest. He resisted making a move toward her to cover her with the crocheted throw, which always lay neatly folded at the bottom of their bed. Still shaken, not sure of what next to be prepared for, he waited until he heard the sounds of her even breathing before he went back to the living room.

The unbroken glass had rolled under the chair he had been sitting in. He picked it up, carried it to the kitchen and put it in the sink. Then he remembered the cigarette. He went down on his knees and felt around in the area where the drink had spilled. The floor felt sticky and unpleasant to the touch. He stopped feeling around for the cigarette butt. He would let the housekeeper find it tomorrow, he thought. Then he listened for sounds from the bedroom. Everything was quiet.

At the polished marble table in the corner with bottles and cocktail mixing paraphernalia arranged on a silver tray, he poured himself a fresh bourbon into a new glass and settled back into the embrace of the wing chair. All the while he avoided looking in the direction of the middle window. After a few sips, the warming effect of the alcohol convinced him that the awful thing had passed. That he had managed to hold at bay the unimaginable.

The sound of sirens woke him from a sleep he may have sunk into for an hour, or only a few minutes. It was dark. He didn't remember turning off the light of the standing lamp next to the chair. Now, he saw that the middle window was opened wider than it had been. A breeze was blowing the curtains toward the room. Red and blue lights made bouncing reflections on the walls and ceiling of the apartment. Insistent, heavy knocks at the door wiped away the remnants of sleep. A scenario, like a movie trailer that had been speeded up, played in his head. He opened the door. Two policemen and two firemen loomed large in the hall. Behind them, heads were appearing in opened doors. Stumbling to the bedroom, his feet got tangled in a bunched up piece of a white garment on the floor.

"Oh, no, no, ,.. it can't be!" the man howled. "No, no!'...There was scarcely a dent on the bedspread, where earlier he had laid down his catatonic wife and waited to assure himself that she had fallen asleep.

"Sir, we are sorry to..." one of the policemen began to say...

"She did it!" he cried. "She really did it this time!"

"Sir, we must ask you ... "

"I was sure I had stopped her!" he cried, explaining, justifying himself to the police at the door. "I really was!"

Then, feeling confused and angry and idiotic, he asked, "How is she?..."

"We are sorry, sir," the second policemen said gently. "But, we must ask you to come down to,...." He stopped himself.

Had the officer been about to say, the husband wondered, to identify the injured woman? Or, what was he trying to say?

"Why did I have to fall asleep?" the husband kept muttering over and over. "Why did I.....? Why, didn't I...?"

The firemen, in their heavy gear, stepped aside while the two policemen supported the shaken man on the way to the elevator. The curious neighbors along the hallway were withdrawing behind their doors.

The body, of what had been his still beautiful wife, had already been removed from the spreading pool of blood on the sidewalk. The façade of the apartment building had no balconies on the street side. It was not surrounded by a spiky iron fence or a well leading to the cellar area. The woman had encountered no obstructions along her fall before she crashed, landing face down, directly under their window of the ninth, the top floor apartment. Inside the ambulance the covered body on the stretcher hardly made a mound. The EMT attendant lifted the part of the sheet that was covering the head. The husband looked at the crushed, bloodied face. He nodded. That was enough. Nothing more was asked of him.

CASSANDRA

1.

The ringing of the phone on the little table by my bed woke me from a deep sleep. Early dawn light peeked between the slats of the venetian blind. I knew what I was about to hear.

"He is gone," my husband said. "At about four thirty this morning."

"About" sounded strange for some reason. There had to have been an exact moment when he was gone.

I picked up my wristwatch, which had fallen on the floor next to a pile of books.

It was five twenty-three.

My husband had received the call only moments before he called me. He made no explanation or justification for not having been at Matthew's bedside at the time of his death.

"I am so sorry," I said.

My reward for having donated so many years of my life to a man who had been my husband was to be chosen the first in line to hear that his lover was dead.

"I'll have to call his mother," he sighed.

Why, I wanted to say. But thought better of it.

Instead, I repeated again how sorry I was.

The woman lived somewhere in Schwarzwald or Bavaria. From what I had heard from my husband, Matthew referred to her as "the gorgon." After escaping to New York "to realize his potential" in the opera world, the son of the gorgon muti had traveled to Berlin once or twice to connect with friends but, he had never gone back home. As far as I knew, his mother had never bothered to meet him in Berlin or, come to visit him in New York City. Would she have stitched pink triangles to his shirts and jackets? I wondered. Was it likely that she would even have any interest in claiming the ashes of her baby boy?

"Would you like me to make the call?" I heard myself say. "I could pretend to be one of his singer friends." Then I asked, "Do you know if she speaks English?" He didn't know.

"I could try to tell her in German," I said. Reminding my unilingual husband that unlike him, I had the choice. My German wasn't great. But it was good enough to anticipate a spasm of glee as I poured bad news into the ear of die Deutsche.

"No, no, I'll manage," he said. "I'll take care of it."

There was a sigh. He hung up.

I felt no sorrow for the man my husband had chosen to be the great romance, his great escape from his long life by the side of his female wife. I did feel sorry for my husband. As sorry as I had felt for him when, not long before he had announced his departure from our life together, our cat had died.

One morning, the cat had crawled in from his usual exploration of the backyards and collapsed, heaving and panting, under the dining room table. He must have ventured beyond his regular route, beyond the last fences, gone out onto the wide thorough fare by the park and been hit by a car. My husband had gathered the cat in a blanket and rushed with him to the local vet.

"There was no sign of hemorrhaging, the vet told me," my husband said when he came back home alone. He was advised to leave the cat overnight. For observation he was told.

"Well, then maybe something can be done," I said, trying to give him a hug.

"What can be done? He was so still, just lying there on the steel table." My husband was weeping, "They are so little. Their insides are so little."

The vet called the next morning. The cat was dead.

That very sweet, gray creature had always belonged to my husband more than to me. I was sad but he was crushed by the death of the oddly unsmart little cat.

I would keep to myself my primitive conviction that my husband's chosen rescuer in his escape from me had been rightfully punished. Because he had lured my man of many years away. Because he had caused me to be ripped out of the cocoon I had been wrapped in. Because he had caused me to be an outcast yet again. Not the outcast pointed at by a German with a rifle, or a Pole sneaking off to Nazi headquarters to seek a reward for discovering another Jew in hiding. Matthew had caused me to be tossed out of the marriage, that in spite of everything, I had wanted to stay in. Now, cruel muter nature had delivered vengeance. I had no problem indulging in a performance of proper, sympathetic noises, while not feeling in the least bit sorry that the life of my husband's chosen one-and-only had come to such a swift and sorry end.

I had to tell the children. I began by calling my daughter.

"No surprise to me," she said. "Papa told me about the phony madrigal tour some time ago." Matthew had gone off to Europe on a chase for a cure.

I was taken aback at first. Then it all made sense to me. Why should I have been included in early revelations of Matthew's illness?

"Does your brother know?"

"Yes," she said. "Papa told us both."

Her father's walking out of our life in that unlucky house, that fancy pile of 19th century marble and brick and stone, in which both parents were, at last, forced to face the crumbling of their, oh, so perfect, long marriage, had been to the grown children, no longer living at home, perhaps a sad, but welcome relief.

My daughter had been attentive to me during those days and weeks when I had first been left alone. When I couldn't believe that anything but a black chasm had opened before me. She had tried to be patient with my wronged woman diatribes. Ever since she turned fifteen, we had had a conventional mother and daughter war-and-peace tugging between us. I had been so young when I became her mother. I used to think we had grown up side by side. I assumed our bond would be that of sisters or girl pals. But, she had grown up in New York, a smart city girl through and through. In her mother's New World, she was certainly the savvier one. When I used to overhear her dreadful giggling prattles with her school friends, I had to admit that in matters of sex she was not the naïf that her mother had been. Still was.

"Mama, you know you have been miserable trying to hang on to him," my very grown daughter would try to console and counsel. "You don't need him. Start living your own life!"

Conventional wisdom was useless to my ears then. I wasn't able to come unstuck from the shame, from imagining pointing fingers and veiled glances of schadenfreude. Staying with him had been about shame. The reason for walking away would have been equally about shame.

My grown-up, independent daughter was a designer working in the theatre. Her own road of work and love affairs was beckoning, unwinding before her. I could well guess the ups and downs caused by freedoms, available to an urbane young woman, not tied down to a husband and babies. Freedoms that I, willingly mired in my romancing of the domestic scene, had never known.

"If you are so desperate for a man in your bed, Mama," my designer kid said, "I'll build you one."

We had both laughed. The wit and brilliance of my grown girl minimized the stain of all those years of marriage and compromises I had looked away from and allowed to happen.

On that note, trying to be racy, I confessed to my daughter a recent one-night stand I had indulged in. That, my sophisticated daughter was not ready to be amused by. When faced with her mother's attempts at transformation from wife of her homosexual father to "gay divorcee," she retreated to a protective shell of prim indignation.

"I am not your girlfriend, mama!" she snapped. "Don't try to engage me in girly-girly bar hopping revelations!"

It was a slap. She had fooled me. She may have meant well, once, but she had led me into a trap with her pep talks. She and her brother had known about the fabricated musical tour. Both father and children had kept information from me. Had I known the real reason for Matthew's travels, I might have kept my cute seduction story to myself. In view of what was taking place in the life of her homosexual father, the witty young woman, who had given her shaken mother encouraging shoves to get away from the soiled old nest, had chosen to turn on a dime, reverting back into a disapproving, scolding child.

Oh, dear, oh, dear! Poor thing! Poor things, all three of them. Because after two years after the end of her parents' marriage, the end of playing the perfect family, I had taken a step or two in the direction of reclaiming me, I had made my husband's grown, independent daughter upset and angry. I ought not to be surprised by any of that. The tyranny of families was only too familiar to me from much of what I had learned from literature and theatre.

"Do you feel sorry for Papa for losing Matthew so soon?" I asked. "Is that it?"

I heard a groan on the line.

"Well, I am not shedding any tears," I said, ready to be done with this conversation. Ready to be done. Period.

A healthy sense of fatalism prevented her father's daughter from being made a fool of.

"Don't gloat, mama," she cautioned her mother. "How can you ignore that it may be only a matter of time?"

2.

Since that phone call at dawn a few days had passed. My husband called to tell me the arrangements he had made for cremation. I never asked about the call to die muter. Maybe he had never bothered. It was not my concern.

Then he surprised me: "Would you mind helping me with a small memorial gathering? Here in our apartment."

The "our" grated on me still. I should have said no. But, there he was, feeling lost reverting to old comforts. I assured my sad former husband that I would try to help. That my sympathy was a lie, I had no trouble keeping under wraps. Why not? The "freedom" he had so pompously gifted me with when he walked out, liked me well. His liberation had been undercut by death. Life and feeling good was on my side.

On the designated afternoon for the memorial gathering, I arrived early at the dark, street level co-op apartment, which my husband had called his "dream apartment," but which Matthew had not found to his liking.

Now he was dead, and I was arranging pate and cornichons from Dean and Deluca on my husband's dining room table for a good-bye meal in his honor. I found a bowl for a cabbage salad and another one for a bean salad. I had bought a poppy seed cake in a Polish bakery on Second Avenue. A bouquet of white roses went into a glass vase I placed in the center of the table.

When the buffet was set, just before the first group of the invited mourners had begun to arrive, my husband placed a framed headshot of Matthew, wearing a Tyrolean hat with a feather, next to the bouquet. In this not too recent photograph Matthew looked healthy, smiling his annoying, pinched smile below his little Hitlerian moustache.

I would play the hostess. As I had done countless times during my years as his wife. I glanced at the table. It looked nice. Red wine was breathing, white wine was chilling in an ice bucket. Matthew's fussy, pretty flowered plates from Bavaria were neatly stacked next to properly arranged silver utensils. A table set for a gathering. A party. Like any other. The honored guest would not be there.

When post separation hurts and rages had begun their fading away, when Matthew and my husband had actually settled into the co-op from a makeshift rental, I had been invited to dinner served on the same plates I had just arranged for Matthew's memorial. Over the table, hung the Tiffany style lamp which my husband had found in a junk shop many years ago. He had cradled it in his lap during a bumpy taxi ride to surprise me with for a special occasion. The fixture wired and rewired had been a constant over dining room tables in our various apartments for many years. Here it was above my head, once again.

Before we sat down to that first dinner I had been invited to, my husband winked and in a stage whisper said to me: "Matthew is an exceptional cook."

"That's nice for you," said I.

After all those years of my parties big and small, of my pate making and bread and cake baking I thought, the lucky man was living with a good cook, at last!

"Yummy!" said my former husband after tasting the first spoonful of Matthew's gluey, chilled carrot soup. "It has a touch of ginger, doesn't it, Matt?"

"Mmm, yes," I mumbled. "Yes…just a hint. Nice."

After the soup, there was a rubbery orange chicken to chew through.

"Absolutely fabulous," my husband said.

There I was. Sitting under my old dining room lamp, smiling, trying to chew and swallow while listening to prattle about current opera transgressions. Between dishing out portions of food and running back and forth from kitchen to dining room, Matthew had been treating us to the dishing of an aging, but still popular tenor and his recent appearance as Cavaradossi at the Met.

"They had to transpose down "E lucevan le stelle" for him. "Did you know that?"

I shook my head. No, I didn't know that.

"It's a wonder his toupee didn't slide off when he fell before the firing squad," the fabulous cook went on.

I looked at my husband. The indulgent smile on his face was the same that used to appear when he listened to the chatter of his little children.

How could my smart, witty husband find the imbecilic opinions emanating from this priggish mouth, below the twitching moustache of this man either sexually enticing or intellectually tolerable?

"Peach Melba," Matthew announced with an operatic flourish, spooning something fruity into desert dishes.

Pour Nellie must be turning in her grave, I thought.

"What a nice way to end a perfect meal," I said.

I had spent weeks and months climbing up from under the shame I had been hiding behind the trimmed hedges, behind the heavy oak doors, behind the scintillating stained glass in the windows of our house. The house was sold. I was gone from it. I was accepting and fitting into the "freedom" of bachelor girl life in my open, sunny, ghost free loft. I had arrived at allowing myself to feel mostly embarrassed for my husband.

I thought of the day when my husband had told me that Matthew had been hired by a madrigal ensemble to sing at a Renaissance music festival in the Netherlands. Engagements in Germany and France were to follow. He was to be gone for several weeks. I was astounded by Matthew's sudden stroke of professional luck. I never imagined that he would ever progress beyond appearances at some cobbled together, temporary Camerata, or an occasional small budget wedding at which the gathering would be treated to his rendition of "One Day my Prince will Come" from a Romberg operetta.

3.

After Matthew had left for his musical tour, my husband began to call often inviting me to evenings out.
"I have two tickets to one of the Stravinsky\Balanchine black-and-white evenings," was one invitation. "Would you like to come?"

We had never missed these performances when the New York City Ballet season was on. When Stravinsky died, there had been a memorial presentation at the New York State Theater. During intermission everyone in the audience had been served little glasses of vodka. Balanchine had offered a toast from the stage. A roar of "Happy Birthday, Igor!" rose from the audience. We gulped, but refrained from tossing our glasses *a la russe*. They were collected on silver trays by ushers going up and down the aisles.

My husband and I continued to arrange "dates." Dinner. Theater. Not unlike our dates when we had been students. Except now we sat in much better, expensive seats. Not way up among the gods. Or standing at the back of the orchestra.

The no longer married middle aging New York City couple, adjusting to separate lives, discussing performances, never ceasing to talk mama and papa talk about their children. The children. Grown-ups. Self involved. Detached. Accepting the parents' break-up. Not surprised. If they had been saddened, it was for the passing of their mostly good childhoods.

How does the lyric to the song go? "Everything's different, nothing's changed. Maybe, only, slightly rearranged." Wise, wise Stephen Sondheim.

It was odd, I remember thinking, that during these "dates" there had not been any details, or even much general mention of Matthew's European musical tour. Did spending chaste evenings with his former wife keep my husband from straying, while his lover was away? And, why did I go along? The dates during our student days had been full of future plans. In our new lives, we often dredged up lists of regrets and the wrongs we had subjected each other to during our years together. It was not surprising. It was sad. It was funny.

One midday I had asked him to come to lunch to a new eatery in Soho. It was a rainy day. I stood at the window looking out on the wet street, the gray skies. He was very late. It was not like him. I waited. I called. After several rings, ready to hang up, I heard fumbling and the crash of the phone followed by a slurry "Hello, hello…" It was obvious that he had been drinking. And he was crying.

"I am so sorry," he blubbered. "I screwed up… I am so sorry."

I didn't like to hear him cry like that.

"Why, why did this happen?" he sniffled.

"What in the world happened?" I was sure it had something to do with Matthew. He probably had met someone on his tour.

"What has happened?... You can tell me!....." I felt like a little girl who has never heard her father cry. We had cried together after fights. This was different. "Please, please, tell me...!"

"I was so wrong," he went on. "I thought it was just fine to... I am sorry.... I am sorry..." He didn't have to spell it out. They broke up, of course.... That's what happened.

"Should I come over?" I asked, feeling more curious than anything.

"No, no," I heard him blowing his nose. "I want to get out of here."

"Then come here," I said. "And don't have anything more to drink," I added. The line went silent. He won't show up, I thought.

But he did. Stumbled in half an hour later, disheveled, red in the face. The walk in the drizzling rain had sobered and calmed him a bit.

He sat on my new Italian couch. He was still sniffling. I gave him one of my handkerchiefs. I had made strong black coffee and handed him a mug.

It was then I was told. Matthew had not gone on any madrigal tour. He had gone to Switzerland to visit a clinic in the Alps that promised an immunotherapy cure for AIDS. When the promise of the Swiss cure evaporated, Matthew had been told of a doctor in Berlin. That came to nothing. He was really sick now.

He was "coming home." Home! To the "home" a few blocks down the street at the corner of the park, away from my new home and new way of being. What part was mine to play now? If and when I made proper polite visits to the home of doomed Matthew and the man who used to be mine. Was I to play helper to my, now needy, former husband? Talk about this or that new pill that I had just read about in that morning's Times? Or slide into distracting chatter, pretending everything was normal and encourage talk about the latest transgressions against missed high Cees, imperfect tessituras and tenors in toupees?

"If you need... " I was about to ask.

He reached for my hand.

"I thought it was just fine to walk out on you, to leave you alone," he said. "Now, I will have to get ready to be alone..."

"Now, stop," I said. "Matthew is coming back. He is not dead yet."

For several weeks after his return from Berlin, Matthew existed in a fluctuation of good days and bad days. There were small stretches of time when he could almost believe that he was going to "lick this thing," as he expressed it. But it didn't take long before he was overcome with sudden cold sweats, rashes, gastric problems... I don't know if he was aware that my husband kept me informed. During the phone calls I listened, interjecting reassuring noises, while thinking, "Frankly, my dear...I don't...."

One evening Matthew had begun to vocalize, which led to a bout of unstoppable hiccups.

My husband called to tell me the next morning: "By ten o'clock I took him to emergency," he said.

The hiccups persisted for two days and nights. Then Matthew developed a fever. By the time it had climbed to 106, he had been wheeled into an isolated cubicle.

"As though he smelled," my husband was bitter. "As though he had the plague."

He does, I wanted to say. He did. Stink of cheap cologne. After your trysts you would return with Matthew's fetid smell wafting around you, sweetheart.

"Poor little guy," I said.

After the hiccups and fever were brought under control, Matthew developed a bronchial infection. My husband and friends were told not to visit. When he was allowed to leave the hospital at last, he was armed with new pills, new hopes, and strict instructions to stay away from vocalizing.

I stayed away from the sick place on Washington Square.

The afternoon of the designated memorial gathering, the mourners, men and women of various ages, were members of Matthew's musical cliques. People embraced, sighed, and made the expected remarks.

"I am sorry",.. "Poor Matt, ..he didn't deserve this"…"I didn't even know he was sick,"

A young man in a frilly pale blue shirt and matching tight slacks, hair pulled into a ponytail began to sob. "How long had he been infected? "

The question hung unanswered in the air. An older man with a little pointed beard and a tightly buttoned suit and bowtie embraced the crying young man and murmured phrases of sympathy. It was at that moment that it occurred to me, with a chill, that Matthew may have been sick before he and my husband had ever hooked up.

"He had been so happy to find the love of his life," said a large young woman dressed in a voluminous flower printed dress. Before plopping down on our old Victorian couch from Brooklyn, she grabbed Matthew's portrait and clutched it to her breasts.

"He is here with us," she sobbed. "I can feel him in this room. I can feel him in my heart."

My husband looked uncomfortable. He extricated the photograph from heaving bosom and clutches of plump fingers and put it back on the buffet table.

A man, dressed in white jeans, a red bandana kerchief sticking out of one back pocket, another member of some ensemble thing Matthew had been performing with, delivered a short "we are here to celebrate the life of" eulogy.

After a moment of silence, glasses were raised. "To Matthew", ... "A fine and loyal friend..." "An exceptional musical artist,"... "So great to work with ..." "He will be hard to replace,"... etc., etc....

Then the mourners arranged themselves near Matthew's white upright piano with a Spanish shawl draped over it. The man with the little beard sat down to play an intro. The group dove into an arrangement of Dido's solo lament from Purcell's "Dido and Aeneas." Matthew, in drag, had performed the role of Dido in some church basement. I didn't know where his ashes were going to be "laid in earth."

I busied myself with the buffet. I made room for the clusters of grapes, the box of chocolates, some fruit and cheeses the mourners had brought.

The remembrances and embraces subsided. Wine was poured. The apartment filled with a subdued, but familiar sound of scattered party chatter. Which my husband seemed to have no problem joining in.

Sex is a willful act. The lusting for it is not easy to sustain when the object of desire is decaying and emits unpleasant smells. Maybe my husband had had enough of his darling Matthew. Maybe being a domesticated gay lover was not all that different from being a domesticated heterosexual husband. Nobody loves so much that they are not relieved when the diseased, lingering body no longer makes demands. When it is transformed into the purity of ashes.

My husband, being the host, looked well and trim, and so nice in a white collarless linen shirt, thin, a little flushed perhaps. I mused on the new way of our knowing each other that was falling into place. Maybe we had come full circle into turning some corner, around which conventions of shame and regrets did not reside? And I looked at the man I had lived with for almost thirty years, and, I wanted not to be in this place, for this occasion, on this day of my life. And my thoughts turned back to the interesting boy I had met when we were new and innocent with each other. When we were simple and naïve and loved each other and were full of plans and promises.

4.

On one of the first days in my first year at the art school, wandering in hallways, peeking into classrooms and studios with canvases on easels and stands with clay models and rooms with drafting desks I inhaled the wonderful smells of linseed oil and turpentine and the grey smell of modeling clay, when in one open space I came across an exhibit of works by students from various classes. One large painting of an old man stood out. The man was leaning back in an overstuffed easy chair, legs spread apart, the belt buckle of his pants unclasped. He looked sleepy, indolent. His face, square jawed but slack, his eyes focused somewhere beyond the gaze of the viewer. The predominant hues of the painting were mottled rose and ochre, the colors of a fading chenille bedspread or an old lady's bathrobe.

Not long after seeing the painting, I noticed, pinned to a bulletin board in the student lounge, an announcement for auditions for performances of three one act plays, the school's drama club was planning to present. It was then I recognized the name of the student, who was to direct Chekhov's farce "A Marriage Proposal," as the painter of the old man.

I knew the play about a manipulating peasant father forcing his marriageable daughter upon an unwilling suitor. I might have decided to audition no matter what. What better way to wiggle myself into social activities at the school than to join the drama group? My curiosity about the painter decided it. I was the first to arrive at the audition, held on the stage of the auditorium.

After I told the nicely square shouldered, slim hipped boy in dungarees and white tee shirt that I very much wanted to try out for the play, I jumped in with, "I was very impressed with your painting."

Behind his horn rimmed glasses his gray eyes twinkled.

"It's a painting of my grandfather," he said.

"It was by far my favorite piece in the whole show," I said. I flattered, but I was telling the truth. I wanted him to be interested even before I read the audition lines. I wanted to be chosen for the play.

He probably had not expected to be surprised by a girl in a peasant skirt and a braid hanging down her back to show up to audition for a part in a classic Russian farce.

I wanted to tell him that I had acted in high school plays in Stockholm. That just before I had arrived in New York City, I had played a villainous, dark Eastern lady who loses her knight to the pure Nordic blond in an adaptation of a classic Swedish chivalrous poem. In the last minute I decided to skip that part of my resume.

The talented painter of the pink and ochre grandfather portrait handed me the typed script with the audition scenes marked.

"Let's give it a try," he said. There was something about the way he said that. It was as secure as the way he had posed the body of the old man and played with and controlled the colors in the painting.

We read two little sections together. He read very well. First, the part of the father. Then he switched to the suitor. On the stage of the rather musty, gothic auditorium of the art school, I gave an anxious, but convincing reading of the part of the sacrificial bride, tossed between two farcical and crude men.

Two days later the cast list for the three one-act plays was tacked on the bulletin board in the student lounge. My name was listed for the Chekhov play. There was a date for the first read through. There were contact numbers. I met the other two actors. An industrial design student had been cast as the suitor. A rather dour older student, a man on a GI bill, was to play the father. The after school rehearsal schedule was easy. I volunteered for scenery painting. And I made my own costume. Not all that different from what I had appeared in for the audition.

We rehearsed in the afternoons and evenings. We gave three performances. They went well. I liked the applause. I was nervous and happy and more and more interested in my attractive and smart painter/director.

He began to ask me out on "dates." That word, meaning rendez-vous, I could not get used to in my new forays into the colloquial quirks of the English language.

He knew a lot about theatre and music. It impressed me. He invited me to a ballet performance of a Bach concerto choreographed by a George Balanchine for the New York City Ballet. Although I had seen ballets at the Stockholm Royal Opera, I had never imagined that ballet could be anything but girl dancers in tutus and toe shoes, extending acrobatic legs high in the air. Mostly to the tunes of waltzes and mazurkas by Chopin or to melodies from Viennese operettas. In those performances, the main function of the male dancers was to hold and steady and lift the girl dancers. Their reward was to get a few minutes of showing off time of gymnastic leaps across the stage.

I had never seen a ballet dancer flex a foot, or present hard edged, un-pretty gestures. Set to baroque or classical orchestral music, in these performances, that my smart beau introduced me to, I learned to see the music of Stravinsky or Honneger in the angles of the dancers' bodies and in the choreographed patterns on the stage.

And then, the smart boy asked me to a big Winter Festival dance that was held annually toward the end of November at the school.

Even in our special little circle of art students whose smart enthusiasms reached beyond what canvas and brushes and paints and charcoal and pencils on paper could do, this boy was special, special. I wanted him to stick around. I needed him to stay interested. I needed him to stay seduced. I needed a special dress to wear to the dance.

One of our drama group regulars was a student from a well healed family. In an apartment, which could have housed five or six students, he lived by himself. He had painted all the walls and the floors black and threw big parties. He had records of all the current and many past Broadway musicals. If he felt the parties in his apartment were not enough to impress his friends, he would buy up blocks of theatre seats and invite us all.

One night there must have been six of us in the first row of the mezzanine, watching Mary Martin flying through the air as "Peter Pan."

Until I was accepted at the art school, I had been deprived of so much since my arrival in New York City. I was thrilled to be included along with my special boyfriend in what I thought was a flamboyant clique of theatrical artist friends. The rather desperate rich boy, who wanted to please all his friends, had seen a self-portrait I had been painting. I had clothed myself in a Polish folk costume. Voluminous, lacy white blouse, topped by an embroidery encrusted vest, a thick wreath of field flowers on my head and a suggestion of ribbons tied at one shoulder. My brush strokes were quick and fresh. It wasn't a bad piece of student work. When I was little, before the war, I had seen these costumes worn by Polish girls marching along on national holiday parades on the streets of Kraków. I had longed to own and parade around in such an outfit. Even if I had owned one, I would not have been able to wear it. During the war, being as invisible as possible was the way for a Jew to try to survive.

"I really like your painting," our well-to-do art school friend said. "Would you let me buy it?"

I never considered being paid for making artwork. Money was earned working in a factory, or in a clerical job, or from selling things in a store. Or at a flea market. Not from making paintings one loved to do. I also thought it would be crass to sell a painting to a fellow student. But this offer seemed like the well timed magic lifted right out of a fairytale. I so wanted to have a new dress for the dance. To look special for my smart cavalier.

I sat in a black sling chair in our friend's all black apartment and said:

"I am embarrassed to accept money from you. But, if you really like the painting, I am willing to,...I would like to sell it to you."

He reached for his wallet and counted out $25.00.

At Orbachs on 14th street such a sum was enough to buy a white moire satin dress. It dipped to a V in front and back. The elbow length sleeves were edged in mink. I loved slipping into a garment that I did not have to pin and baste and sew on my old foot pedaled Singer. Just wiggle into the ready-made silky shape and primp in front of the small mirror in my dreary room.

On the night of the dance, my date climbed the six flights of stairs to our tenement apartment to be met by me in my elegant new dress. He looked distinguished in a dark suit, white crisp shirt, a striped bowtie. Under his jacket peeked a green silk vest.

"You look beautiful," said my date. "Very elegant."

I did surprise him. He had only seen me in my usual home stitched, gathered skirts and bohemian blouses or black sweaters. And the costume I had made for "A Marriage Proposal."

He brought me a present. Not the corsage I knew girls expected from a "date" before a dance. This too, I knew from American movies. He handed me a box with a bottle of perfume. I had a split second of worry. Maybe he had not liked the way I smelled, when he had kissed me after our ballet evening.

He had other silly concerns; "Will your parents think this is a proper gift?"

The name of the perfume was "Tigress."

"My parents don't have to know," I giggled. "Besides they are not home from work yet." I didn't say that I cared not a whit for what my parents thought. About anything.

Right there, by the door, I unscrewed the top of the perfume bottle and sprinkled "Tigress" into the deep V of the décolletage.

He was proper and interesting, handsome enough. And, he was funny and very smart and more and more promising.

At the November dance, we looked and were looked at as a pair that belonged together. By Christmas time we were lovers.

At the gathering in the apartment on Washington Square in New York City, the mourners began to heap their plates. There was plenty of wine to pour into crystal glasses. The memorial for Matthew was turning into simply another lively party in the West Village.

Because I had taken strides away from mourning for the death of the married life, that ended on that fading afternoon in that oppressive Park Slope house, I had come and brought food and drink, and helped serve it in his ground floor apartment on the corner of Washington Square. The apartment he in his desperation to find a nest for himself and Matthew had settled on and tried to endow with charms it did not have. Now there would be ghosts.

I had to get out of there.

I gave him a quick hug.

"Thank you," he whispered embracing me. He was trembling. "You have been so good. Thank you."

During the short walk back to my own place, I couldn't help thinking;

How many of these musical friends of Matthew's, putting on proper faces for the occasion, chomping on buffet snacks, may be wondering who among them might be next on the gay death list. Articles of new horrors were a constant front page topic, comparing the disease to the Bubonic plague. The infections that attacked homosexual sufferers at unexpected turns. The blindness, brain tumors, the cancers, the paralysis, the blood and shit....

And worst of all, the pathetic springing up of support groups and AIDS "awareness" marches, and the impossible, occasional glimpses of hope. And, for those who had the courage, when not supervised by guardians, who still had the wherewithal and the means, suicide.

And, my daughter's Cassandrian phrase curled like an imaginary ribbon above my head: "Don't gloat, Mama. It may be only a matter of time."

WINE BAR

1.

In the bathroom in my new space, where there were no ghosts in the walls, I showered, washed my hair and doused myself in perfume. It was a ritual cleansing of that afternoon's event and heaven knows what else. I put on tight jeans and a white silk blouse and added a string of pearls. I headed for the new wine bar, which had just opened around the corner from my loft.

I had hardly settled on a barstool and ordered a chardonnay when a young man moved from his seat to the seat next to mine.

"You look like you have always been around money," he said.

I was a little taken aback by the straightforward, crude pick-up line. I shrugged. I smiled. I had been hoping for something to take me out of the "celebrating the life of" event, but I did not expect such quick evanescence. As though I had dropped an Alka Selzer into a glass of water, and whoosh.....!

I took a quick look at the boy. He must have been a baby at the time of my poverty stricken and difficult early years in New York City. He had a broad grin, bedroom eyes he must have worked on to perfect. His brazen look followed the string of pearls that was half in half out of my slightly unbuttoned silk blouse. He was nicely dressed in clean pressed jeans and a Western shirt. A preppy looking jacket. No tie. His pale brown hair, soft and straight, fell down sideways over his forehead and eyes. On his right hand, the tip of the index finger, about three quarter of an inch was missing. He noticed that I noticed.

"I had an accident," he explained. "On my Hog." He was about to explain what he meant by "my hog," when I chimed in:

"I most certainly do know that "hog" is an affectionate name, for a Harley Davidson motorcycle."

"I like the way you talk," he said. Treating me to a broad dimpled smile. I wondered if he thought there was money in my voice, too. I liked his Midwestern, gritty drawl. A darling, wounded, American working class child. I liked him.

He was from Detroit, he told me. From a large Polish family. I said something about having once lived in Poland. He told me his grandpa had been in the Army.

"Yeah, he was there. Fighting the krauts."

"Normandy?" I asked.

"I don't know much about that shit," he said.

I thought it best not to expand on that line of conversation. I sipped my wine. He sipped his harder drink, whatever it was. With a beer on the side.

He put his arm around my shoulder, "What do you say we blow this joint?"

Not sure at all, I said, "Sure, let's do it."

"My place is not far from here" he said, mentioning an address nearby. I was surprised. I had him pegged as "bridge and tunnel" not a Soho resident. He added, "But it's a mess." Maybe the "mess" was a girlfriend or a roommate.

Solving the problem, I said. "I live right next door."

He paid the bar tab.

Before we arrived at my building he asked.

"Do you have any beer in the icebox?"

We stopped at the Korean's to pick up a six pack.

At home I put the "brewski" in the Sub Zero "icebox."

"I am impressed," he said, strutting around the loft, popping the tops of two Budweisers. We toasted each other with the cans.

"Have you read all these books," he asked looking at the two wall-to-ceiling bookcases.

"Not all," I said. "But many."

"I read westerns by Louis L'Amour," he said.

We kissed. Even with beer on his breath he tasted sweet. We groped. We dropped our clothes on the way to the bed. We fucked.

"What a sweet lady you are," the big strong boy kept whispering. Surprising me with his response to my affection, rather than my probable lack of sexual prowess.

"Lips," he whispered. "You have a hungry mouth, lady Lips."

"Will you be offended if I talk dirty?" he asked.

"Talk whichever way you want," I said. After he mumbled some unintelligible street language sex phrases into my ear, I giggled. "So, what was dirty? It's bawdy talk. Like in Shakespeare."

"Lady shall I lie in your lap?" Hamlet asks Ophelia, I couldn't resist instructing the boy from Detroit.

"You are a pip, lady lips," he laughed. A coarse, guttural and sunny laugh, that rose up from the recesses of his belly and chest and shook his substantial, young body.

There are ways to seduce which enhance the dropping of garments and tits cascading out of a bra. There was more kissing. There was affection. I liked his sweetness and his basic approach. But, he was too quick. Even after another round of his un-circumcised penis inside me, I didn't come.

"I have a small dick," stating the obvious, he sounded apologetic.

"What you do with it is magical,'" I sighed. I lied.

He lifted me up on top of him. This time I was ready. I shuddered and came ahead of him.

In the morning, I left him sleeping in my bed while I tiptoed out to shop for food. On the way back in, I half expected him to be gone. He was there. With a towel wrapped around his waist, he was lounging on my new couch.

"I was hoping for breakfast," he grinned.

I had guessed what would suit him. I heaped a plate with three fried eggs, sunny side up, big, fat slabs of thick bacon and fried potatoes. There were brioche rolls and French butter from Dean and Deluca. He ate with gusto, washing down the food with two of the remaining cans of Budweiser left in the "ice box" the night before.

I had gathered up his jeans, his shirt and jacket, before I stepped out. He had not worn any underwear.

He finished his large breakfast, belched, apologized, said "thank you" and dressed.

The Polish boy was a surprise. Our lovemaking had been clean and fresh and young. More like a sporting event in broad daylight than a determined one night stand in the dark. The presence of this boy, the unexpected sweetness of our tumble in the bed, felt as if a blessing had been bestowed on me.

Could Niania, the imperfect guardian angel of my childhood, have sent a gutsy Polish angel my way, to help me thumb my nose at the "celebration of life" that I had left only a few blocks away from where I lived. But very far away from my life.

At the door he boy kissed me on the forehead, on the cheeks, on the lips. I slipped a piece of paper with my phone number into one of his jacket pockets.
He slapped my ass.

"Ta-ta, fancy lady lips," he said.

The door closed behind him.

He was gone.

ATTACK

1.

The morning I got the desperate call, only weeks had passed since his fatal diagnosis.

"My head is splitting"...he could hardly get the words out. "I tried to stand up," he moaned. "I couldn't...I can't stay upright... please come over... please help me..."

Since Matthew's death he had developed a habit of calling me every morning. Just to talk. Or make one of our "dates." On this beautiful spring morning, hurrying to his side, there was no longer any doubt that the disease had made a new selection.

Somehow, he had been able to get to the front door of his apartment, unlock and leave it open. I found him collapsed on the bathroom floor, moaning, still holding a toothbrush in one hand and with the other clutching his head. I managed to raise and lift him to a standing position and help him to the couch. I covered him with a crocheted throw he always kept draped over an armchair. Even though I had been in his apartment quite a few times during the past year, I had always avoided the bedroom. This morning the bed was a disheveled mess. The sheets had been pulled away from the mattress and trailed on the floor. How long must he have been thrashing, trying to kick away the pain, before he gave up and left the bed. I grabbed a pillow and fluffed it up, about to position it under his head.

"No," he whispered, "No"...

"It hurts less when I lie very flat." I tossed the pillow onto a chair. "I have called the doctor's office," he said, through clenched teeth. "We have to get an ambulance."

I made the call. It didn't take long before we heard the approaching siren.

The two EMT workers, making me think of actors in a weekly television series, lifted the moaning, sick man onto a gurney. A short ride in the enclosed, well equipped medical vehicle, with ECNALUBMA spelled backwards on its roof, so that it could be seen from the air. No angels hovered over this sick transport. The siren's sound was muffled on the inside.

When I gave the ambulance worker in charge the name of my husband's doctor, already known as specializing in the AIDS epidemic, I was confronted with the anticipated questions;

"Is the patient your brother?"

"No," I said, "He is my husband."

"Did he get sick from a transfusion?" came the next question. "From needles?"

"No." I said. "No..."

I hesitated before adding. "He is a homosexual."

If the EMT medic entertained further thoughts based on this information, he kept them to himself. He returned his attention to the clipboard where he wrote down vital medical information.

The ambulance drove silently the short distance to the hospital emergency entrance.

The sick man was lifted from the gurney onto a bed in a cubicle in the emergency ward. He was docile, moaning... An orderly came in and helped him out of his shirt and pants. He had no underwear on. He was helped into one of those hospital gowns, in which modesty and decorum are virtually impossible. I turned away, sparing myself the view of thinning buttocks and dangling member. It had been more than two years since I had seen him naked.

He shivered under several layers of hospital blankets. He kept raising his arms pressing fluttering fingers to his temple, as if trying to erase or push the pain into some far away recess in his cranium. In light of this punishment, which was only just beginning, my moments of murderous rage toward him and his betrayals came to seem paltry and small. Sitting by his side in that dreadful cubicle behind the green curtain, my only wish was for help to appear and gouge the pain out of his body.

Orderlies and nurses came and went. They pulled aside the curtains, peered in, nodded in my direction. Now and then one of them shone a flashlight at the sick man's closed eyelids and didn't do much else. After a glance at the chart clamped to the railing at the foot of the bed, I noticed that they all tried not to come too close to him. My husband had told me that during Matthew's hospital stays, he had been aware of the staff avoiding contact with the patient as much as possible. Before Matthew's sickness and death, the disease had been an abstraction to me.

The sick were anonymous numbers. Out there somewhere. Existing in articles in newspapers and reports on television. They were stories about stricken homosexual men. Nothing to do with women. Nothing to do with me. Now, because of my husband's determined step into gay life, one story was stretching out before me.

I left and walked into the hospital hallway. Here and there, I heard moans from beds that had not been rolled into a cubicle, like the one my husband had been deposited in. I came upon an empty waiting room. The television set, suspended from a ceiling fixture, was tuned to a channel showing a monster truck rally. Trucks equipped with giant wheels were climbing upon and crushing an endless variety of smaller cars and trucks. The sound was turned off.

I left the waiting room and noticed a fat nurse in a smock printed with some colorful dabs had walked into my husband's cubicle.

"Please, give him something," I begged. "Can't you see that he is in terrible pain…His head …" The gruff nurse, with her plump hands encased in green plastic gloves, inserted a thermometer in the patient's ear.

"He has a fever of 106," she volunteered. "But we can't issue medications without the express authorization of his physician."

My husband let out a moan. His eyes were squeezed tight. He seemed to be shrinking, evaporating right under my eyes. I put my hand on his burning forehead. He flinched. I was glad that he reacted.

"Why isn't the doctor here?" I was desperate. "He was supposed to be here when we arrived."

"The doctor is on rounds," said the nurse. As if she were reporting that her boss was taking a meeting. "He'll be here as soon as he is able."

I could not get used to these current get-ups in American hospitals. The quiet nurses I had known after the war, when I was getting over my concentration camp tuberculosis in the sanatorium in Sweden, wore prim starched white caps and proper wraparound white aprons and blue uniforms. They did not behave as if they were inconvenienced by the needs of the sick. They had not only been efficient and hushed, but attentive and angelic.

What did all of that matter now? How had we, how had I, come to this moment by this cubicle with the vile green drapes, with hospital attendees who did not attend. Who wore ridiculous, cheerful smocks splattered with cartoon characters.

In the two years that had passed since the end of our marriage, I had become used to our separation. During those early days and weeks, I had seen nothing but blackness ahead. A road with a skewered perspective leading into nowhere. In the nights wartime memories had invaded my dreams in a way they had not done for a very long time. And, then, while his Matthew was sick and dying, I became for my former husband a trustworthy, familiar comfort to reach for.

Maybe I had become an extension of his worn and steady purple velvet chair. The chair that had gone with him from our house to his apartment. The chair, in which he sat and swiveled and chewed on the end of his pencil, and hummed and murmured to himself, while crafting one after another the children's stories he had become so admired for. And that he had always read to me as soon as he felt he had arrived at a successful ending.

I was surprised how little he had really sorrowed for the death of his darling Matthew. Perhaps his absence from the bed was less missed than his absence from the kitchen. Because soon after that ridiculous memorial gathering in his dreary apartment, my husband began to take cooking lessons. I had listened, bemused and tolerant, when he called to report on his progress in the culinary school.

"Today we made a very proper French potatoes au gratin," he reported.

It had been one of my Julia Child standards.

Another day he had left a message on the phone, "Can you believe it?" he giggled. "Today I prepared a very delicious filet of sole."

One of my failings as a cook was that I could not stand either eating or preparing fish.

After several weeks of cooking lessons, my husband felt ready to invite a group of six for dinner. He had asked me to arrive a little earlier than the other guests.

I was just about ready to leave my apartment when the phone rang.

"Where are you?" he cried, "I am going crazy!" I hated that phrase. It had been a constant with hysterical Matthew.

"I am not sure I can do this," my husband, the newborn chef and host, sounded as desperate as a kid who had invited an important professor or boss, or his mother, to dinner.

"Calm down," I said. "I am on my way."

"How did you ever do it?" he cried before we hung up. "All those parties! All those years!"

I was curious about how he would handle his first attempt as a dinner party host. But what was putting a smile on my face during my walk over was the giddy memory of a couple of evenings earlier. Of my ride to City Island on the back of the Harley, with my arms wrapped tightly around the hefty middle of the Polish boy from Detroit. In a crowded eatery by the water, surrounded by clucking sounds of moored boats and rock music blaring, we gorged on lobster and ribs and drank beer.

"This is eating, fancy lady," my guy had laughed, and burped. Butter and grease dripping from his chin and his fingers, "This is living."

I left the inert, sick man in his curtained cubicle. In a visitor's lounge, again painted the same color of prescriptive green, with another television set suspended from the ceiling, a young couple in jeans and tee shirts with cutoff sleeves showing matching tattoos of the name of a popular rock group on their arms, sat close to each other in plastic chairs, staring glassy eyed at the same monster truck rally. This time with the sound on. On the payphone I dialed my son's number in Boston.

"Hello," his voice cloudy with sleep, answered after several rings. It was past eleven o'clock in the morning. His band had played the night before. He had gone to bed at four.

When I had called right after his father had been diagnosed, he had blurted his impatience in a voice tinged with resentment, even accusation.

"What am I supposed to do? How am I supposed to react to such news?"

I reminded him that he and his sister, as soon as they knew about Matthew's illness, had never had any doubts that their father was doomed. I was the one who had pushed those thoughts aside. I was the one who kept mouthing reassurances. Not everyone who had been exposed was stricken. The disease could be fooled. It might just hover somewhere in their father's vicinity and never erupt and attack.

Then my husband had begun losing weight. A ring had slipped off his finger one morning and disappeared down the toilet. He could no longer postpone making a doctor's appointment. What was coming could no longer be pushed aside. He was calm and collected when he called to tell me. From that moment, I knew I would not be able to avoid being thrust into his certain, steady descent and exit. And the seesawing between anxiety and anger and hope of grown children and friends who would foolishly be trying to talk themselves into the anticipation of news of medical break throughs.

During this call on the pay phone in that institutional putrid green hospital lounge with the noise of crushing metal of the images on the suspended television set, I screamed into the phone: "Papa is burning up... I don't know what to do... I can't find his doctor... I think he is dying."

"I'll leave as soon as I talk to the guys," said my son then. Now, sounding determined and wide awake. The band would have to find a replacement bass player for that night's gig.

I was sorry for the boy. Sorry that he had parents who had come to this. Sorry that he had to drop doing what he had worked hard for and cared about to be interrupted by filial duty. My daughter was working in a theatre upstate New York. Her brother would call her and pick her up.

That sweet boy. At the age of six when "A Hard Day's Night" opened I took him and his sister to an afternoon screening. The theatre was packed with teeny boppers like his sister. Through the unending screaming of the girl audience my son wept bitterly during the entire showing. A few nights later his father took him to an evening show with adults in the audience so that the boy could watch and listen to his idols in peace.

"Please, drive carefully," I begged, sounding idiotic.

I thought of James Agee's novel "A Death in the Family." It had been a birthday present from my husband the year it was published. The same year our boy was born. In that story the young son receives news that his father has become gravely ill. Fearing he will not arrive at his father's side in time, he speeds. The car veers off the road and crashes. The dutiful son dies in the wreck. The father recovers. He's alive and well when he attends his son's funeral.

What the hell was I doing here? How had I arrived at this new horror in my life. I had never wanted to be a divorced woman. I had cancelled the slick lawyer when my husband got sick. Now, divorced or not, I was on a fast track to becoming the widow of a man whose name was going to be added to gay death of AIDS statistic.

When I went back to look at the face of my feverish husband, his eyes were closed. Those cute, small eyes behind glasses, I had loved. The eyes that had sparkled with intelligence and wit. The fever was giving his face a gray, oily look. Since his diagnosis he had been keeping me informed of his minor health problems that came and went. I had avoided volunteering to go with him on "routine" doctor visits. From the Matthew days, he did have a leftover small clique, from which someone was usually available to take him. He continued to work at his desk and in his purple chair.

At last a doctor made an appearance. A young man, his blond curly hair cut in a neat, polite trim. His hospital coat white and spotless. The stethoscope around his neck. His ID tag in place. I don't know if he had seen this patient before.

The young doctor pulled on those nasty, green elastic gloves which made a snapping sound. He shone a beam into the clouded eyes and listened to the heart of the sick man, who didn't budge, only emitted a slight moan.

"His head aches, doctor, ...I know that. And the fever... Can't something be done about.... Please, help him...! Please help him not to hurt...Is he dying?!" Was this doctor, or anyone in the medical profession, faced with yet another case of AIDS, simply ready to go through the motions? But, really giving up! Was the doctor gay himself?

"You can see that he is in very bad shape," was the cool straight forward answer. "Beyond that I can't make predictions."

Tests were coming next. The shivering, half conscious sick man, moaning in pain, was transferred from his bed to a gurney. With a nod of permission from the doctor I followed behind it into a huge elevator. The door slid open. The doctor and I walked through an icy corridor, toward a room with an MRI machine. My husband was eased onto a kind of tray that made me think of an adult version of a baby scale. This contraption was propelled very slowly into a humming giant cylinder, a kind of pristine culvert. I watched his brain being photographed in cross sections from many angles. Which were the folds and crevices of matter that held wit and sweetness, I wondered? In which crenellated sections were hidden the collections of duplicity and lies? Later, projected onto a light screen my husband's brain looked like a butcher's chart. I thought of the occasions, I had ordered cervelle de veau in a French restaurant.

The diagnosis was spinal meningitis. My husband was not returned to the holding cubicle, but wheeled to an isolated room on a high floor of the hospital. He was put on an iced mattress and hooked up to strong antiviral IVs. I asked for the telephone in the sick man's room to be activated. Soon there was a call from my son about to pick up his sister at the theatre.

"Mama, hang in there," he said. "We will be with you in a couple of hours.

Before he hung up I heard him say, "I love you,"

Not much later, their semi conscious father, before falling back into slumber, did manage to treat us, our reunited sad trio, to a grimace passing for a smile. It was obvious he did not have the strength to care. But whatever was dripping into his arm must have had painkillers galore in it. His previously shaky hands stayed at his side and did not reach up to his head as before. Two registered nurses made frequent visits to monitor the gradual, very gradual lowering of the fever. If any of the staff had been puzzled by the presence of two grown children and a wife by the bedside of a homosexual man with AIDS, their demeanor stayed discreet and stoic.

In the young doctor's face, I searched for signs of reassurance. I wished to hear words that said: Everything will be fine... Everyone gets sick now and then. The children's father will bounce back hale and hearty. What he did say was:

"He is very sick. Your children ought to stay close. Just in case..."

A cot was brought to the hospital room. The three of us held vigil overnight. I dozed in a chair. My daughter and son took turns taking little naps on the cot. We took turns getting watery coffee and candy bars from the machines in in the hospital corridor. In the waiting rooms the black and white television screens dangling from the ceiling at last, had turned black. Nurses came and went during the night. They checked the patient's temperature through his ear and were careful to monitor the IV drips. He never stirred. I did not say much to the nurses. They were doing their jobs.

In the morning the doctor and a nurse came back. After a quick look at the passive sick man, he listened to his chest and heart. He looked at the fever chart at the bottom of the hospital bed. The fever had broken. He seemed surprised, when he told us that the patient was indeed much improved.

"If this continues," the doctor said, "We will take him off the iced mattress later today or tomorrow." The patient would have to stay sedated for the next few days. But, for now, he was slowly, slowly inching back. I noticed, again, that his hands were staying still, not reaching toward his head.

"You are all here," my husband's voice was very weak, but he managed a real smile. A practical nurse in a smock patterned with pictures of Charlie Brown characters brought a breakfast tray. He was able to drink some apple juice through a straw. All three of us crowded around the bed with tentative encouraging smiles on our faces. We were exhausted, but felt that life was returning to the sick room.

I was sure that the children's thoughts were rewinding to the activities that were tugging at them and demanding their return. I checked with the doctor.

"He is not dying," he said.

"You know you should not have to be doing this, mama," said my daughter. I rolled my eyes. "But, I have to get back....We are in tech...."

" Go," I said. "We can't all three sit around here staring at him."

"Are you sure, Mama," my son whispered. "The guys can do without me for a couple of nights.

"Yes, yes! Yes. Go...!" I hated playing noble, mater familias. "You go! Both of you go!"

I knew then, I knew, that their father was not going to simply drop dead. He would hang on for a while. His slide down the slope of the disease was going to be a gradual descent. More likely his body was to be chipped away from him sequentially. He would dwindle in small or large increments. Neither I nor his children nor his friends were going to be spared the graphic reality, the clatter of paraphernalia, the obstacle race with pharmaceuticals. And the futile hopes that were bound to grip all of us against our wills.

After the children left, I stayed in the room for a while. The man in the hospital bed was asleep. I put my hand on his forehead. Then I felt mine. Our warmth was equal, normal. His fever was way, way down, maybe even completely gone.

Mama was not required to do any of this. My daughter was right. But she and her brother had left. I had to be at least halfway connected to their father's care. For today. For now.

I went to a hospital administration office and put in a request for a practical nurse to stay with my husband at all times. I filled out and signed forms. I supplied a credit card. The efficient young woman at the desk, this one dressed in a white hospital coat, with an ID tag pinned to her chest, said;

"There will be a nurse available within the half hour."

"I would be most grateful," I said, handing her a piece of paper. "I can be reached at this number any time."

I walked through the revolving door into the light of a glorious noontime in May. With every part of my body I breathed in the air of the New York City spring. I had not been obliged to be that well behaved, proper woman doing that decent thing. I knew more of the same was to come. For the moment, I walked out through the revolving hospital door, grateful to step into daylight and sunshine.

TWISTS AND TURNAROUNDS

1.

More than a year had gone by since he had been diagnosed and the recovery from his bout with spinal meningitis. That young doctor had frankly admitted to the family that he had not expected him to pull through so well. Then he had directed us to consult with a doctor, who was becoming known as the New York City AIDS specialist. This small young woman crippled from birth, lived her life in and directed her medical consultations from a wheelchair. After the meningitis attack, my stricken husband had become her patient. He had fought off pulmonary infections, gastric incidents, eye infections, hiccups which lasted for hours and left him exhausted. From these he had come home to his apartment with prescriptions for the latest and newest potions and pills designed to hold back the inevitable.

Aside from the official medications, there was the well meaning stream of good advice from gay and straight friends and acquaintances. That emotional soprano from Matthew's memorial gathering was a constant. She often dropped in, bringing with her the latest New Age clippings and articles. Her standard advice to the sick man was to drink plenty of bitter green tea and eat freshly steamed broccoli every day. Another visitor came with news of a doctor in Northern California, who was soon to announce a definitive cure. One guy, who was not himself sick, but active in Gay

Pride and AIDS Awareness, brought a thick, holistic something available from GMHC.

"Mix it with orange or grapefruit juice," he suggested. "It won't taste too bad."

My weary husband nodded and grimaced and reached for his checkbook to make a donation. He shoved the putrid looking, thick, yellow-green concoction in the refrigerator.

Once, while he was dozing, I ventured into his studio. A rather cramped little room, adjacent to the bedroom. By the street level window, on his drawing table, still the same one that for so many years had been nestled next to mine, I could see stacks of tracing paper, covered with preliminary drawings. Even when Matthew was caving, in and out of the hospital, my former husband was able to gravitate toward his purple chair with his spiral notebook, chew on his pencil and mumble the words to his next story. Or, find concentrated focused time to spend at the drawing table. After this latest hospital stay he was, once again, returning to furious productivity. He was completing work-in-progress and he was accepting new work. Hoping to beat the real deadline.

His "dream apartment", as he had called it, was on the ground floor of a prewar building on the corner of Washington Square Park. It had taken him a long time to find the place.

"It has wonderful dark wood moldings and details and beautiful polished oak floors," the liberated man had announced to me, as if he were a kid who has been sprung from his mother's home at last. "There is a working fireplace."

Before our Brooklyn house, that showy but unlucky place, had even closed I had, without hesitation, put money down on my nice, small, open loft space in a newly converted 19th century former leather factory in Soho. It was on the third floor, not huge, but light and airy, with high ceilings and exposed pipes and brick, with some walls sheet rocked flat and painted gleaming white. The tiled fireplace was new and in perfect working condition. Tall windows faced east. Across the wide street, I had a view of preserved, restored, made into expensive living spaces cast iron Beaux Arts buildings. If artist squatters had not taken charge twenty or so years before I became a resident, all of this beauty would have fallen before Robert Moses' wrecking balls.

The lofts in the front of my new residence had been designated for working artists. Until my lawyer presented and cleared everything with those in the city government who were required to approve my artist status, I worried that my portfolio of children's book illustrations and textile designs would somehow not qualify. Later, after I had settled into my new surroundings, I discovered a loose interpretation applied to these "Artist in Residence" rules. A couple of hair dressers bought the apartment next to mine. Calling themselves "hair sculptors," presenting a portfolio of photographs of their contributions to fashion shows had qualified them for AIR status.

My fresh, new living space brought promise for the new girl in town bachelor life, I had never known. I was going to be a Manhattan woman, dropped into a perfect address. Friends came over to admire the place, anticipating dinners and parties. Some of that would come. But, on the day movers crowded in with the divided leftovers from my long Brooklyn, married life, I sat in the middle of a dump of stuff I did not want and sank into a deep hole of misery. Then I decided to rid myself of most of it and start anew.

I had claimed my right to hold on to the classic Victorian loveseat we had found years before discarded on the street one night. It had a back of two never especially comfortable concave hollows and a raised oval in the center. Long before the acquisition of our status house could have been imagined, we had struggled, laughed and lugged that loveseat three flights of stairs to our first Park Slope apartment. Some of the horsehair stuffing had been peeking out of the worn upholstery. I had covered it in corduroy and later recovered it in chintz, fitting and securing the fabric on the armature with upholsterer studs. We had laughed at but treasured our reconstituted find. We prided ourselves on ingenuity, which in our early life together had substituted for lack of money. In the house it had become a professionally reupholstered in crimson velvet divan that we placed in the master bedroom. Its chief use had become a seat where to put on shoes. Mostly we used it to toss clothes on when we were undressing.

When my husband confessed that Matthew really wanted to claim the loveseat, that it ought to go into their Washington Square home, I became determined to hold on to the old relic. I tried to will the Victorian thing to fit into my new interior. In the end, I had to admit that my many years of attachment to this uncomfortable old sitting object were gone. Loveseat, indeed! Two friends of Matthew's came and were incapable of maneuvering the sofa into the elevator in my building. They gave up and had to struggle carrying it down three flights of steep stairway. Matthew must have enjoyed planting his ass on the crimson velvet for a time. It fit right into the fusty, darkrooms on the ground floor of the Washington Square apartment. Having felt not quite comfortable in the leap into his new life, and guilty for leaving me the way he had, my husband forked out money for sleek Italian seating arrangements suitable to my brand new, downtown New York City quarters. I was ready to plunge smartly into the "freedom" that he had "given me" that late afternoon in the living room of our fancy house on the tree lined street in Park Slope.

My husband may have thought his new home to be perfect. Penniless Matthew did not. Even though he had wiggled into comforts he could not have provided for himself, he grumbled.

"How come she ended up with such a cool place, and we are living here, in an old lady apartment on the ground floor, listening to drug dealers outside our windows?"

Then, the happy couple discovered that the real estate agent had lied. The fireplace, a great bonus for any New York apartment and attractive eventual resale did not work.

None of this mattered for long. My husband's perfect find, his supposed "dream apartment" intended for the domesticated romance of two gentlemen of Manhattan, had become, in a very short period of time, a cluster of small dark rooms suitably set up for dying.

"After you two separated, Mama," my son rued, "Papa hasn't been very lucky."

A time came when the children and I had to convince their father ought not, should not, be living alone. He needed help with daily chores. At first he put up a fight, yes. But he could not sustain it. He liked service. He liked giving orders. He liked being free to work.

My husband had met Jerry, one more actor who was working as a server at some cocktail party. He was yet another small man, in my husband's seeming preference for small men. He was of some undetermined age. No longer the young boy he pretended to be, dressing in very tight tee shirts and short shorts, held up with a variety of suspenders. Pigeon toed, he wore high tops with knee socks. His feet were too big for his small stature.

Jerry turned out to be an oddly useful and proper gentleman's gentleman. He took my husband to doctors' visits. He kept a neatly organized notebook of prognoses and advice and the measuring out of pills and concoctions. He did the laundry. He ironed. He fancied himself to be a creative cook. His grilled vegetable sandwiches on toasted rye or wheat bread, with trimmed crusts, cut into triangles, made one think of cocktail snacks. The toothpicks he stuck in the centers of his creations made me worry that the sick man would choke on one. One midday I arrived finding Jerry spooning brown beans onto a serving of spaghetti carabonara.

Jerry may have aspired to playing Tennessee Williams' Gentleman caller, but he would have been better suited playing a munchkin in an off-off Broadway version of The Wizard of Oz. He installed himself in the spare room on the other side of the kitchen. For someone his size, he had a surprising deep voice. He was often annoying telling anyone who would listen about the times he had three call backs, almost got the part. Then didn't. When he worked, it was as an extra on film shoots or commercials. He liked to knit.

"I can hear the needles clicking," my husband would say. "Even when his door is closed."

We made fun of Jerry behind his back. But, we were grateful for his presence.

And he was grateful for the permanent/temporary employment.

For months my husband was to sit in his purple velvet chair receiving a constant stream of visitors. In the rather hermetic, close-knit field of books for children, he was a name. People came to be nice, to be "supportive," to be seen in his presence.

They came with smiles pasted on their faces, bearing false hope, boxes of baked stuff from neighborhood bakeries, paper bags of fresh fruit, flowers with stalks tightly squeezed in rubber bands and wrapped in cellophane from Korean grocers.... There were times when I was able to convince myself that all of this attention being paid to the sick man was more than a prolonged wake.

One hanger-on, a minor journeyman writer of children's book texts, mostly series written to order, who lived nearby, who was not really a friend, but who had sometimes been included in the food and drink laden Brooklyn parties, came so often that it was becoming obvious that the writer used this sad excuse for a salon, simply to be seen among the visitors from publishing houses. My husband knew it. The children knew it. I knew it.

One late afternoon I had dropped in to coincide with a visit from my son and his fiancée. The doorbell rang. Cheerfully barging in, interrupting our family gathering there was the hanger-on again. He had visited only the day before. He had not called to ask if it would be all right to drop by.

"I brought you my latest," he said. "An advance copy of 'The Secret Boys' Club." Fresh off the press." He handed my husband a paperback chapter book.

"I dedicated it to you," the writer beamed.

Perhaps encouraged by his latest post hospital return and improvement in health and the presence of the still constant former wife and attentive children, the man in the purple chair, took the book without a "thank you," or even a slight attempt to flip open the cover to arrive at the dedication page. With a fluid theatrical gesture, as if he were tossing a Frisbee, he threw the paperback volume in the direction of a flat magazine basket. The book missed its target and landed on the floor with a quiet thud. Then my husband swiveled in his purple chair to face his unctuous visitor.

"Don't come here anymore," he said. "You bore me."

The stunned writer stood there for a moment, frozen, looking at me, at my son and his intended, hoping for reassurance, an explanation, for something.... Pretending to soften the blow, trying to signal with the roll of my eyes, a gesture with my hand, that the sick man didn't know what he was saying, that he had to be tolerated, I escorted the unwelcome visitor to the door.

"Bravo, Papa," his son applauded his father. His fiancée and I joined in. All three of us gave in to bursts of nasty laughter. The writer was a bore. And we all agreed that Papa need not waste precious time, politeness and tolerance on a hanger-on, who used our sad family situation as an opportunity to network in juvenile publishing.

The interims of returned health did not last long. Infections and fevers and respiratory problems came and were dealt with. There was a less dramatic than the meningitis recovery from a minor bout of a chest infection which had sent him to the hospital for two days. When he recovered, he was able to go out again. I got us theatre tickets. We went to restaurants. Sometimes with one of the children. Sometimes with friends. Sometimes he and I alone. He wanted to do these things. But so often he couldn't sustain the pretense and caved, shrinking into the theatre seat, or chair or banquette in a restaurant only to stare at the plate before him, saying nothing.

"Why can't you be a little more....?" I tried cajoling.

"A little more what...?" he challenged. "What should I be?"

"Think of the sick people, who are all alone," I surprised myself by blurting the obvious. "Who don't get to be taken to a show or dinner in a nice restaurant?"

"Why should I be so grateful for having a plate of steak frites at "The Union Square Café?" he snarled at me. "I am dying. Just like all the others."

I couldn't come up with a counter argument. Besides questioning my own participation at these pathetic tries to sustain him. And why? He had brought this avalanche of horrors on himself. My remarks were making a fool of him. Making a fool of myself. He was right. And I was succeeding in making myself one of the gray ladies.

Kaposi's sarcoma arrived. First on his back and chest. Those spots he could hide. Then the blemishes, like love bites, kisses and tooth marks of death, started proliferating on his neck. Those were harder to disguise. Finally some popped out on his cheeks and jawline. There was special make-up available from GMHC. It was too obvious and insufficient as camouflage. He grew a beard and wore high collars to cover up the blue/purple marks. He was still able to guard his secret at a time when in the news media Kaposi's had become a daily word.

Even though it was known that we were living apart, we were still invited to functions together. If he was up to it, we went. At a party one evening, a woman, who knew us only slightly, and did not know he was ill, asked him, "Why the beard?"

"To distract from the gray in the hair on his head," I piped in with an explanation. There was no reason to let this casual acquaintance know how much I questioned my choice to play the part of the wifely cartoon.

And then my husband went through a period of no attacks at all. He gained weight. No new blemishes were springing up. He felt well. We were alone one midday. Jerry had prepared lunch for us and gone out. Sunshine was streaming in through the slatted blinds. There were stacks of completed pictures neatly arranged on the architectural chest of drawers next to his drawing desk.

"What I would really like is to take a trip back to Venice again," he said. "Will you come with me?" he asked. I was stunned.

The year before we separated, without much ado, we had decided to hop on a flight to Venice in mid July.

On the plane, in coach, the drink cart had just passed. We were holding hands and toasting each other with prosecco in plastic cups, giddy and happy to have given in to an impulse and gone with it.

We had started chatting with a middle aged couple from Missouri who were sitting on the other side of the aisle. This was their very first trip to Europe. Or, as the man called it, first "across the pond."

"Are you two on your honeymoon?" the woman had asked.

"We have been married for twenty seven years," my husband answered. With pride I had thought at the time. Pride and a sense of wonder in his voice.

I thought of the afternoon of the day after our arrival. We had been surprised and delighted to run into a couple of illustrators from London we knew. The four of us had sneaked into Wagner's Palazzo. It was supposed be closed for mezzogiorno. But the guard had dozed after eating his midday pasta and neglected to lock the entrance gate. He was slumped in his chair with a napkin sliding down the front of his unbuttoned uniform jacket. His empty dish and utensils were still in front of him on his desk. We were fortified by our own lunch in the restaurant known for its Fegato alla Veneziana and local wines, near the spot where Katherine Hepburn had fallen into the canal during the filming of "Summertime."

If my husband and I had been alone, we might not have been so brazen. But, bolstered by the presence of the other two and carafes of vino, we acquired the courage of a gang. Trying to keep a lid on our giggling, running on tiptoe around the exhibits of scores and Wagnerian memorabilia in glass cases and paintings and photographs on the walls, we gave ourselves permission to play informed hooligans. In the height of summer, we had no trouble falling into the spirit of a personal Carnavale. We left the Wagner mansion as we had arrived, sneaking by the guard, still slumped in his chair, still deep into his post pasta nap. Visiting flies had assembled to buzz and take advantage of leftover smears in his pasta bowl.

We had followed those antics with bringing bouquets of red and white roses to San Michele to place on Stravinsky's grave. I was prepared with a silver flask of vodka in my handbag. We toasted Igor out of plastic cups and were proper enough to deposit them in a garbage receptacle on the way out of the cemetery.

It wasn't until later, when time had passed and much in our life had been turned upside down that I came to think of that liquor infused, Venetian frolic as a feverish preamble to the dissolution of our life together. On that trip, I had taken a picture of my husband in a straw hat, sitting in a beach chair on the Lido, pointing into the far distance. To some Tadzio he pretended to have spotted? And in spite of everything I knew, or suspected or decided to ignore, I never wanted him to stop being my husband.

"Are you sure you wouldn't rather go with someone else?" I asked.

He shook his head.

"No" he said. "Don't be silly. I want to go with you."

Venice, the elegant, decaying amusement park for pretenders to art and music and theatre, always about to sink into the polluted waters of its canals. Where one can lose oneself on a dark, murky street, turn the corner and find oneself on an open piazza in blazing sunlight. Venice is the one place where one need not apologize for being a tourist. Should I go with my dying husband and play his attentive tourist wife? Just a nice American middle-aged couple flying in for a quick respite in Venice in summer. Oh, God! If I agreed to his wanting to play "death in Venice," what did I expect to reclaim. Or make better?

A homosexual man who wishes, oh, so much, to marry a woman, is a Venus flytrap. He gets what he wants. And he sucks, if not exactly the life, the fighting spirit out of the woman. He may have done that. But not without a tacit permission from me. Why place the blame on a seducer, who really had not been all that skillful at seducing. He had not been some diabolical

Don Giovanni or Faust. He had never pretended to be. I ought not to blame him for what I could not possibly have known as a newly arrived girl on the shores of New York City. He was smart, and proper and nice. I wanted for him to stay in my life. He persuaded himself I was sexy. I wanted to be wanted. Not to live with my parents and spend my life around their dreary cousins and their "nasze." He was a visa to my new life. Whatever he may have imagined that he wished for, I had wanted the same thing. I had continued to hold on to the belief that in the life we had built together, we were comrades, pals, partners…..and lovers, who slipped away from the scimitar of treacheries hanging above us, and paved our own road with determination to prove something, anything… what?

Having walked away from six childhood years of facing death from Hitler's killers and cooperative Polish Jew haters, I should have known how to take advantage of remembering. Then, I had had no doubts about my Niania's Catholic certainties. I believed in the benevolence of the Virgin and the Rosary, the blessings of the Christ Sacred Heart, the protection of angel wings and medals of saints around my neck. I had waited for that shot. Had been ready to accept it. The Nazi had pulled the rifle away. The bullet had not pierced the back of my skull.

That single memory ought to have laid the foundation for a life of wiser decisions and courage and independence. Not such soft capriciousness and small fears I had caved in to. I should have known better. I should have taken advantage of my darker knowledge. I didn't. I didn't know how. I had been sucked into a promise of benign, conventional cozy domesticity. What foolishness. What fraudulence. What capitulation...

And, now that the man who had been my husband, the father of my, of our children, who had betrayed me, was hurtling toward certain death. I had recurring variations of thoughts during which I could not stop imagining that if I returned to my simple beliefs of long ago, I might bring to the sick man a saintly serum, to keep at bay, or even reverse the forward march of the disease. I didn't want to go back to being his wife, no! But I would put all that magic to use and save him.

When we had been constrained by lack of money, when we had been innocent and stupid, we had been smarter. With money had come choices. With choices had come arrogance, petulance and daring. I wanted to believe that for almost three years, the living of our separate lives, the illness he was rotting away from, was a wicked charade, an illusion we had been indulging in. And, if I could, I would rewind us back to those simpler, early years, to return us to "stupid" innocence.

I would go to Venice with him.

ENCOUNTER

1.

On the terrace of our hotel, at a shaded corner table, I was sipping morning coffee. I drank it accompanied by a glass of *sambucca con la mosca*. The sweetish anisette flavored liquore always served with a coffee bean, the little "fly" swimming in the transparent thick liquid was an aperitif, not a morning drink. But I had no trouble convincing myself it was no more than a sugar substitute added to strong black coffee.

Cool breezes blended with the cloying smells of the Venice waters and with the July perfume of flowering acacia trees. The clatter of breakfast service competed and blended with the clucking sounds of moored gondolas, poking each other. On the other side of the Canale Grande loomed Santa Maria della Salute. Much to the amusement of our two young children, when the family had taken a first trip to Venice together, my husband had christened the baroque marble edifice with its massive circular curlicues, "The Noodle Church."

I had been very quiet when I slipped out of our pale rose colored hotel room and left the man, who used to be my husband, still asleep in the twin bed across from mine. I did not close the door behind me until I had assured myself that his feeble snoring breaths were going to stay with him for a while. I was glad to be alone.

Before we left New York, I had gone with him to see his brilliant physician, known as "Doctor Death." From her wheelchair, maneuvered like a warrior vehicle, she dispensed unflappable advice and diagnoses and handed out prescriptions for whatever medications were currently available to prolong the life of her doomed patients. I was taken by surprise when I focused on the pristine soles of the Mary Janes on her little feet. Facing forward on the extension shelves of her wheelchair, they made me think of the rigid legs of a doll. These little shoes will never get dirty or wear out, I mused.

The doctor suggested that my husband needed iron. That he ought to try to include eating a serving of liver on a regular basis. He had made a face:

"Doctor, would it matter?" he said. "Shouldn't I be allowed to eat food that I really like"?

She shrugged. Smiled. Agreed. And gave him, gave us, the go ahead for our Venice trip.

Three days before, at Kennedy airport, though it seemed to me as though a more considerable amount of time had passed, we had joined long lines of summer travelers waiting to check into coach class on the Alitalia flight. A large tour group of couples from somewhere out of the heart of America, women and men both, dressed in matching, oversized shorts, baseball caps, supplied with blue vinyl carry-ons stamped with the word Buon Viaggio Travel.

Among these ruddy, healthy, noisy Americans on a trip, perhaps planned for a long time and, at last, coming to pass, the mood of celebration was palpable.

Casting a glance at my husband, so thin and pinched and uncertain, clutching his small shoulder bag with his medications, I had made a quick decision.

"Come," I took his arm and pulled him away from the check-in line. "This won't do."

Upgrading was no problem. Seats in *Prima Classe* were available. With our new tickets in hand, we were ushered away from the coach class crowd toward Priority. My husband, had refused the service of a wheel chair. But, until the flight was called, he did not object to the luxury of a Milano designer chair in the First Class Alitalia lounge. He had sipped a Pellegrino, while I helped myself to a gutsier choice of liquid.

After pre-boarding, we both sank into the ample seats, as comfortable as LA-Z-BOY loungers. There was instant service of prosecco. I took a glass, while the flight attendant reached over and placed another on the fold-out tray by my husband's window seat. He ignored it. As soon as I had gulped my drink, I downed his as well. Then, I had gone to peek from behind the curtain separating first from coach to watch the crowds piling into the back of the aircraft. Amid the usual warnings from the PA system and from flight attendants cautioning passengers about the bins above their heads opening accidentally in flight, Coach Class was filling to capacity with elbowing passengers struggling with carry-ons, fitting or not, into overhead compartments. No inconvenience stopped the party noise rising from the crowd, whose jollity was unstoppable. I was reminded of our happier trips to Europe. When we had been back there, giggling, uncom-fortable, paying for our drinks, anticipating the moment of unmooring and the improbable lifting off the ground of the immense metal container we had wiggled ourselves into in anticipation of the promise of wonderful somethings we were going to experience after we were deposited again on earth far away from home.

In *Prima Classe*, my husband, in the oversized bedlike airplane seat looking more shrunken and sickly than ever, reached for his zipped up pouch of medications. When the flight attendant brought him a glass of water, I couldn't avoid noticing the veiled look of suspicion she gave him. A look, I feared would lead to questions. But the proper airline attendant kept her cool and opted for discretion. I drew a sigh of relief.

After swallowing the prescribed doses from his collection of plastic drugstore vials, the sick man had tucked in his thin frame, almost obliterating himself under the pillow and ample Missoni blanket, and promptly fallen asleep.

I chose to stay awake. I was not going to waste the flight in First Class Alitalia on sleep. As soon as we were in the air and the flight attendants were up on their feet, I lifted my glass, requesting "un poco di piu, per favore." And I indicated that the man next to me preferred not to be wakened for dinner.

While my impulse to switch to *Prima Cla*sse had been for the sake of his comfort, of course, I couldn't deny that I had wheedled a perk for myself as well. Why not? He owed me. All of it. The ubiquitous scented hot towel preceding dinner served on an ample tray on china with real flatware and linen napkins. After an amuse bouche, there had been pasta nera, followed by osso buco. And a choice of vino rosso or bianco in stemmed glasses. After the main courses, the meal had been completed with cheese and fruit, a tiny tiramisu, followed by a snifter of cognac. For the rest of the flight, my husband had only come awake long enough to swallow his next cocktail of medications, drink some water and throw a cloudy look in my direction.

Our midmorning arrival in *La Serenissima* under the blazing Adriatic sun felt not all that different from other arrivals in this place. We only had carry-ons. This time I carried both our traveling bags. At passport control, once again, I noticed, or imagined questioning looks directed at my husband. But he had slept for the entire trip and was not unsteady on his feet when we were helped into a water taxi.

Having preferred the comfort of the open bar to resting in my reclining seat, I only returned to doze in it for part of the time during the flight. But, stepping out into the midmorning breezes and sunshine, I was not sleepy or tired. I was high. My travels to Europe as an American have always seemed like a triumph. Arrival at a temporary choice of study or play. Not the old thing in which my life had almost ended. Not my parents' even older old things. Just a place where I could spend money, nod to culture and speak languages. Which were not required for getting a job or applying to a school, but pleasant luxuries to play and dance with. And I liked the moments of arrival the best. The moments that beckoned and stretched before me and carried with them promises of surprises. I turned to look at my husband, leaning back in the motoscafo seat. Glum, pinched, his skin blotched and sallow he was staring straight ahead. Oh, God! In the sunlight beaming down, augmented by the shimmering reflection from the water, he looked frightful. I knew then that on this trip the promise of surprising delights were not in the offing.

Getting out of the water taxi, my husband, trying to step onto the hotel landing dock, did stumble.

The hotel attendant, ready to great us, steadied him and asked, *"Si senta male, signore?"*

"E solamente un po' stanco." I moved in, folding my hand to my cheek, pantomiming need for sleep.

The familiar reception rooms of the hotel were filled with their ubiquitous giant urns of glorious, fresh flower arrangements. When, in the past, we had attended a work related function, in a hotel suite or a banquet hall featuring similar floral bouquets in big vases, my husband always muttered, "Funereal, isn't it?" At such moments, I was prepared to roll my wifely eyes, equally irritated and amused by the anticipated remark delivered on cue. On the morning of our arrival in this hotel, in this city, there it was again! This time the "Funereal isn't it" quip wasn't amusing. It was ghoulish. It gave me the creeps.

We checked in at the reception desk, presented passports, were wished a happy stay in Venezia, and followed the hotel attendant carrying our two traveling bags to the iron cage elevator.

The room we entered, papered in pale rose tinted wall paper depicting frolicking Commedia characters, so very similar to the one we had stayed in during our last happy visit, underscored the sadness and weirdness of our current arrival. When making the reservation, I had been careful to request twin beds.

"I am tired," my husband said, as soon as we were alone. He claimed one of the twin beds and, in spite of all those hours of sleeping all the way across the Atlantic, he was asleep again within minutes. Oh, well, oh, well, well! So be it!

Let the man, who used to be my husband, go on sleeping in the imitation 18th century twin bed in the rose colored room in the elegant hotel in Venice. He is very sick and knows it. We both know it. We both know he is dying. I will wake him up at some point. As much as his strength will allow, we will walk around and try to play tourists and recall and look, once again, at beautiful stuff we had seen before in this legend of a city. Or, if he chooses to stay asleep, I may end up having Venice to myself.

Out of one corner window, I was once again treated to the view of the baroque curlicues of Santa Maria Della Salute. I had nothing left in my account to expect salvation. My good grace with the Holy Mother, I had squandered over a long time. And still continued to waste.

And so I began my Venetian morning with the pouring of a bubble bath in the deep marble tub of the hotel bathroom. Then, I opened the door and perused the goodies in the well stocked mini bar. Let morning coffee wait, I thought. Let me linger in perfumed froth sipping a little something from a crystal glass. And, when the water begins to cool, I will turn the faucet and replenish the cooling water in the tub with a stream of acqua calda. And, perhaps, when I rise from my soak, I will refill my crystal glass with another splash from the minibar to replenish me.

On the terrazzo, I finished my coffee and sambucca con la mosca, and a sweet pastry. I left and took the elevator up to have a quick peek in our room. I tried poking the sleeping man to reassure myself that he was not comatose. He didn't stir. He slept. Again. Still. There was a slight, unhealthy rattle coming out of him. But he was just plain asleep. I let him be and left the room.

From the moment we had stepped out of the sundrenched Venice morning, into the rose colored charm of the hotel room remembered from a past romantic rendez-vous, I was confronted with my misguided giving in to my dying no-longer-husband's wish to have me come with him on this trip. The rather grotesque obligation of stuffing the few days of our stay with the culture gawking of tourism were stretching before me.

In this city, with its rich history, famous for gaudy revels, theatrical traditions, constant reminders of death, where we two, in better times, had indulged in innocent, inane, pleasures of tourist discoveries, how would this fading man, with his halting steps recreate the sightseeing through the claustrophobic dark calli and splendid, open piazzas? What did I really owe this dying man? Agreeing to help him stage a fitting last act for himself. And why Venice? A flamboyance I associated with Venice never really suited him. And at this point, was he even strong enough to sustain interest in what he had imposed on himself? And on me? I could not free myself from the sadness and the regrets and barely disguised anger.

Now, three days had passed since we had come to Venice. Three days of my trying to keep afloat the reason for being in this place with conventional tourist determination.

I walked out of the hotel, into the Venice of late morning. Crossing the already tourist and pigeon clogged Piazza San Marco, I ducked into and meandered through quiet dark calli and crossed little bridges, at last emerging at the noisy, busy Rialto with its stands laden with fresh fruit and vegetables and flowers, and constant displays of gaudy and gilt Venetian Carnavale and Commedia kitsch. I listened to hawking and bargaining in Veneziano, which is its own language, and which my school Italian did nothing to help me understand. I did my touristy poking around without desire to buy anything. I smiled and shook my head when long nosed, grinning masks or glass objects from Murano or lace edged linen handkerchiefs from Burano were thrust at me by pleading black clad old ladies. I even passed on bouquets of flowers. I feared they would wilt during my stroll back to the hotel. Anyway, fresh flowers in small vases were brought to our room every day by the hotel staff.

The time moving past mezzogiorno made me think I had better begin to wander back to the hotel to check on the man I had left sleeping in the twin bed across from mine.

When I found myself passing Harry's Bar, I decided to step inside. The place was dark and cool and almost empty. It seemed to have been paused. I sat down at the bar. The bottles on the shelves before the mirror behind the bar facing me sparkled and enticed with jewel-like liquid temptations, guaranteed to take the edge off ruminations and dis-appointments. Renowned Harry's is not fancy, but within its walls, remains the breath and presence of decades of celebrated literary wit and alcoholic chatter and quarrels. I ordered a Bellini.

A couple of barstools away from mine, a man alone looked in my direction, hesitated for a moment, then slid off his seat and moved over to plop down on the barstool next to mine.

I had put on a black cotton dress and a hammered gilt necklace, a bit heavy for the rising heat of the day. I had taken off my wide brimmed straw hat and put it on the bar. My long, dark hair was loose. My feet were sweating and seemed to have grown larger during my wanderings. I considered slipping out of my sandals.

"You are an artist," the man sidling up to me said. "I can tell."

He was drunk. I could tell.

American English. Tourist from somewhere out West I guessed. Stopped at Harry's Bar because he had read about the famous place. Maybe he was part of an "elder" tour? He had managed to sneak away to play by himself. "I.E," I had heard it was called. It meant permission for a bit of "independent activity," away from the organized activities of the group. He wasn't bad looking. With salt-and-pepper hair, even slumped, leaning on the bar, he presented a suggestion of tall and lanky. He was wearing a rumpled beige shirt, jeans, no socks on his feet in fine loafers. Not the ubiquitous Nikes or Adidas, so constant on the feet of American tourists young and old. He was an American in Venice. And he was going to have fun.

Why should a guy assume that being taken, or mistaken, for an "artist" was a flattering come-on? Why wouldn't, "You look like a restaurant hostess," or "You look like a nurse" not be as good an opener?

Should I let him think I was Italian? That I did not understand English? I dropped that idea.

"I don't know," I said. "Am I?"

"And you probably like fantasy," the man plowed on. "Am I right?"

He was ridiculous. Sounding as if he had prepared an outline out of a pocket guidebook of pick-up lines.

"I don't know what you mean?" Trying to sound my most earnest, I said. "What sort of fantasy?"

"Sex, dear lady," he whispered, looking around the empty Harry's Bar. No need to worry about being overheard. "Sex with some... "

"Oh...Now, I see what you mean," I interrupted. Not caring for further clarification. "No, actually, I like nice, normal sex."

He laughed. He seemed to have found my straightforward response seductive. Maybe he even thought I was negotiating.

Oh, God, I was weary. Allowing myself a witless flirtation. Falling in step with the comings-on of a drunk. Questioning the reason for finding myself in this part of the world, on this barstool, at this moment...

"You exude sex," the seducer persisted. "You must know that?"

"Am I supposed to understand," I asked, removing my dark glasses and opening my eyes wide, "that you mean that as a compliment?"

"Of course I do," the man grinned. I couldn't help noticing that he had nice teeth. "But you talk like you went to school with the nuns."

Now, I liked that! That was nice. Why not let him think I was a well brought up, sexy, former catholic schoolgirl. Yes, I had spent time living in the proximity of nuns, but that had more to do with trying to stay alive than with being bien éléve. I finished my Bellini and asked for another. The bartender obliged, placed the drink before me and removed himself into a dark corner behind the bar.

"Are you sure we couldn't go someplace," the clumsy seducer slurred away. "Where we might continue, er, our conversation....and,.. er,..enhance our acquaintance?..."

He attempted to reach for my hand, humming, *"La Ci darem la Mano."* That surprised me.

"I am sorry," I said, moving my hand out of his reach. "I am attached."

So was Zerlina, I thought.

"If I were whoever he is," the drunk went on, "I wouldn't let you out of my sight."

I had to admit that I wasn't having a bad time. Life should be lived like this. Surprising me with the delights of flirtatious, anonymous encounters. Letting drunks young and old in dark bars believe that, of course, I was a well brought up former catholic schoolgirl! Who might, on occasion, indulge in sipping a cocktail and treating a gentleman to witty repartee and a teasing promise of a "fantasy" fling. Had I been drunk enough, I might have given in. I might have persuaded myself to prolong the encounter with the sloppy Harry's Bar Don Giovanni as an antidote to the trumped up patience I had been keeping afloat for the sake of the man I was "attached" to.

Then I could feel the second Bellini kick in, and thought it best to make my exit before the situation got more sticky.

"I must rush back," I said, grabbing my hat, adding, "To him who ought not to let me out of his sight."

Ignoring my bar bill, why not let him pay? I tossed behind me, "Thank you for the libation!"

"Ciao!"

I fled the cool ombra of Harry's into the early afternoon light and heat of Venice. With all that drunken flattery and the two Bellinis, I was a little better prepared to go back to the sick man, maybe still asleep in the twin bed in the hotel room with the Commedia figures dancing on the rose tinted wallpaper. Turning once to make sure the drunk had not hopped off his barstool to follow me, I hurried in the direction of the hotel.

I crossed a bridge just as one of the smaller gondolas was maneuvering through the narrow canal. A young Japanese couple, reclining against red velvet cushions, looking up toward the sky, spotted me on the bridge. Laughing, the young woman waved her bouquet of flowers. Perhaps they are on their honeymoon, I thought, and waved back. The young man lifted the camera hanging from a strap around his neck, pointed it toward me and snapped a picture.

"*Auguri!*" I called before the gondola disappeared around the next bend of the canal. I was lightheaded. I hoped I had made the supposed newlyweds think that they had waved to and photographed a happy Italian woman wishing them luck. They would put the picture into an album of rice paper pages to preserve with many other mementos of their wedding journey on the other side of the globe.

I ducked into one of the darker calli. In these narrow passages the heat of summer was kept at bay by the massive walls that leaned so close to each other, they seemed to want to touch in the middle of the passage. The blue sky was a ribbon curving up high between the dark buildings. Here and there, iron rods were fixed to the walls in an attempt to keep the houses from caving into each other. In my darkest days and nights in Park Slope, I had imagined that the walls of our house, pushed by the neighboring walls on both sides, were moving together to close in, ready to crush me.

My thoughts rebounded to the drunken seducer. Did I like fantasy? Those I was haunted by, I would gladly sweep out of the storage compartments in my brain. Since my long, perfect marriage had crashed and ended, I could not erase visions of my husband lusting for his Matthew as he never had lusted for me. Taking him from behind, plunging his dick into his darling's Vaselined asshole, both of them groaning, moaning, exploding…reversing the position? And, before Matthew, how many other posterior openings and couplings and effluvia had there been in how many crumpled bed sheets. Or, lacking beds and sheets, under bushes in parks, or the toilets in gay bars. What did he do and what had been done to him by this or that rent boy he may have hooked up with. I doubted any of these "fantasies" of mine had much to do with those my clumsy seducer in Harry's Bar had imagined after watching some midnight "adult" video on television in his hotel room. All those things my husband must have been doing, when I was left, so many nights alone, in that house, on that wide street with all those leafy, whispering trees. With only my bottle of vodka as my comfort and compensation.

And yet, and yet, here I was still and again with him. In Venice! As if his tearing himself away from me had been all my fault, my doing, my stupidity. If only I hadn't been a girl newly arrived from Europe, trying to reshape my life away from old world parents, or from the residues of war and from even older shackles, I might not have given in to fashioning romance and falling into the benign domestic prison of the peas and carrots fifties. If only I hadn't been,... If only I had been.... If only my blow jobs had had more finesse...If only... If only both of us hadn't been so skillful at making fools and liars of ourselves for so long. So good at keeping the weight of our marriage from tumbling down the hill,...Jack and Jill, indeed!

Between the moments of anger and contempt and disgust I felt for the sick, dying man, I did indulge in other wild fantasies. I had flashes of hope, wishing to wrap the pitiful man in a shroud of saintly goodwill. That same trust in religious magic, vivid from times long ago on the wartime landscape of Poland, would well up with renewed fervor. If I did succeed in bringing back those beliefs, I might be able to cast out the vengeful demons attacking him. Fury and betrayal would all be erased. Young, innocent versions of the two of us and of our sweet little pliable children would return. Everything good and simple and nice would spread before us. Blue skies and breezes from the lagoon would envelop us in an embrace. We would dance the tarantella on Piazza San Marco and wave to the noodle church and count our blessings. And back home we would bore friends with our anecdotes and photographs of picturesque, unexpected delights. Purified and blessed, my husband would no longer be stricken with the homosexual disease. He would no longer need the ministrations of doll footed doctor Death in her wheelchair.

And then, anger was back. And I hated myself for the dupe I had been and still was, agreeing to go with him on this trip. Let it all be done, I found myself thinking. Let them find the corpse of the diseased sleeper in the twin bed in the room with the Commedia wallpaper in the fancy hotel on the Canale Grande in Venezia.

I "fantasized" talking in halting phrases of broken Italian to Venice authorities, to the doctor and police arriving in the official *vaporetto*. Being comforted. Making calls to New York City. Escorting the casket onto the plane going back to Newark or Kennedy. Or maybe the grieving widow could negotiate a burial spot for her spouse on San Michele? Perhaps somewhere in the vicinity of Stravinsky's grave? With the black draped casket I would, at last, take that funereal gondola ride. Death in Venice? Life after death? In Venice?

I thought of a line from a play by Edward Albee, "All Over." From which I had once worked on a scene in acting class.

In the play a powerful man, who never appears, is dying. On the stage, in the library adjoining the sick man's room, his presence is only conjured by his wife and his mistress holding a vigil. The trajectory of the man's life is revealed in the women's exchanges of confidences …..At one point, the mistress asks the wife what plans she may be making for the future. The wife launches into a long bitter monologue ending with the surprising line:

"And, perhaps, I shall spend Christmas in Venice, where, I hear, it finally snows!"

PALLADIO

1.

ℬack at the hotel, my husband surprised me by being up and showered, and dressed and very much awake. There was a tray of a few breakfast leftovers on the coffee table.

"I see that you ordered room service," I said with surprise and admiration in my voice. He laughed, as if he thought I might pat him on the head and say, "Good boy!"

"They do speak English in Room Service, you know," he said, adding, "Where have you been all this time?"

"I didn't know how long you would go on sleeping, so I took a walk," I said. "I stopped at Alitalia," I lied. "To reconfirm our return trip seats in First."

I could easily take care of that the next time I left him sleeping.

"Are you feeling strong enough for a Venetian stroll?" I asked.

"Yes, I am," my husband said sounding almost perky. "I am still hungry." he added.

"Well, in that case," I said, "Guess where I think we should go?"

For the first time since our arrival, he was not acting like someone supervised and pulled along on a leash. A proper American couple on vacation in Venice, we were going to eat in a restaurant we knew and liked. I embraced his thin frame. Planting a kiss on his forehead, I held my breath, avoiding the fetid smell of the cake make-up, covering the blemishes. I was glad he wanted to eat.

It was a bit of a walk. I thought I remembered the direction to the restaurant known for its Fegato a la Veneziana, the local vinegary specialty of liver with onion and bacon. We had eaten there on our last trip. I hoped it was still there.

I led the way with confidence, only to realize after twenty minutes we had spent twenty minutes walking in the opposite direction. We had to retrace our steps. By the time I recognized the little bridge ahead as the one leading to the restaurant, the sick man was visibly losing the burst of energy he had greeted me with in the hotel room earlier.

The small restaurant was packed and noisy. We had to wait. By the time a table was available we had no choice but to be seated outside, under an umbrella, but still with enough bright sunshine bearing down. It may have been my constant self consciousness, but where we were placed my husband was a sitting duck exposed to scrutiny. In his swiveling chair or on the couch at home in his apartment, with curtains drawn, soft lights adjusted, close to his drawing desk, surrounded by friends who came and went and tried to keep up a sense of normalcy, his thinness, his marked face had become acceptable. In the summer light of Venice it was another story.

Our pretty waitress, golden hoops in her ears, a buxom, luscious presence exuding health and wellbeing did cast a quick look at the guest at the table. He knew it. He knew why he was being looked at. He knew he looked awful. The spots all over his body were covered, but those on his face and neck could not be entirely camouflaged. His fingers kept adjusting his buttoned up collar or moving up to his forehead. The proper cameriera didn't dwell for long on scrutinizing the frail, sickly customer. She took our orders and was soon back with a smile and with tiny tomato tarts, bread and olive oil for dipping and the full carafe of vino bianco I had ordered. He tried little bites of everything and even took a couple of sips of wine from his glass.

The *fegato a la Veneziana* was as delicious as I remembered it. And, obedient to doctor Death my husband did eat well. At the end of the meal there was not much vino bianco left in the carafe I had ordered. There didn't seem to be much energy left in the sick man either. I paid the bill and we made our way back at a cautious pace. This time not losing our way.

Even though he was fading, he wanted to take a step or two along the Riva. We stopped to look across the water toward San Giorgio Maggiore toward the Palladio church. Its illuminated marble whiteness outlined against the perfect panorama of azure sky, suggested a piece of stage scenery which had no connection to my old Catholic, magical thinking. This idolatry belonged to my latter day bow to the admiration of a gorgeous piece of Palladio's classical architecture.

"Do you remember?" my husband asked, smiling. I knew what he was referring to. I did remember.

The first time we had travelled to Venice with our twelve year old son and fifteen year old daughter, we had taken the vaporetto across the Giudecca to the Isola di San Giorgio Maggiore. Papa and the kids were having a great time pointing and teasing, anticipating the fun of seeing Mama stand before and enter the interior of the church she had read and talked about so much at last

"Look, look! There it is, Mama! Your church! For real! At last!"

The dazzling, white marble of the Palladio masterpiece was blinding in the blazing sun of high noon. After we crossed the patterned piazzeta before the edifice, the children and their father stood aside and let me walk up the couple of steps toward the heavy, polished black wooden portal. Expecting weight and resistance, I pushed. Nothing happened. I tried again. The door did not budge.

"Bang on the door, Mama," said my daughter. "Someone will hear you!"

"They must open the door for you," said my son. He was very earnest. "It's your church, Mama!"

No one came. The portal remained shut. The church was not allowing me in. My kids no longer snickered and made fun. Instead my husband pointed his camera at me. With my fists clenched, I raised my arms high, struck an operatic pose of despair and turned a Caravaggesque face toward the camera. That snapshot from many years ago, had been inserted into a family album of travel pictures. It ended in a cardboard box somewhere in a dark nook of a storage space in New York City.

When on another morning during that trip the church door had not been locked and I was allowed to walk into the interior of San Giorgio Maggiore, I had been taken aback by the detached serenity of the white columned interior. I felt as if I had walked into a space designed for a political oratory or for stately theatrical performances, not for the passion of the Catholic Mass the little Jewish me, trapped between Poles ever ready to inform and Nazis ever ready to round up and shoot, who had found in the Catholic country churches by the side of Niania's whispering of her Rosary.

"It IS your church," said my frail husband standing by my side on *Riva Degli Schiavoni*. "It always will be."

"Always " was a word we ought to stay away from, I thought. I said nothing.

We slowly made our way back to the hotel. He sat down on the bed. It was not yet evening. For him the day was done. I watched his shaking fingers fumbling with the buttons of his shirt. He let it drop to the floor. Not bothering to slide out of his pants, he lay back against the pillows.

"Enough Venice for me for today," he mumbled. I took off his shoes.

Our rosy room was bathed in the late afternoon light. Soon the Venice evening would be in full swing. The gondolieri, maneuvering with balletic skills, would encourage their flocks of tourists in their festooned boats to join with them in the *Serenata* echoing along the Canale Grande. On our way back to our rose tinted hotel room with the twin beds, I thought of Venetians and tourists alike who would be heading to hotels and pensiones and homes to finish festive days and evenings with nights of joyous, noisy sex. For me and the man shuffling by my side, doors to such delights had slammed in our faces a long time ago. And stayed shut. our faces a long time ago. And stayed shut.

MEDFORD AND MATISSE

1.

My husband and I are sleeping in a bed with a lumpy mattress under a heavy feather bolster in his grandparents' house up north. Next to our bed in a frilly basket, our three month old baby girl is asleep. There is a loud banging on the door. Two Nazis come crashing in. They grab the baby and run out, laughing, tossing her back and forth to each other like a rubber ball. "Komst du mit, du Judishe schwein," they taunt me. "Komst mit uns spielen." I jump out of bed and follow them, thinking, why isn't the baby crying?

I am running in a snowy field. The Nazis, their rifles and bayonets glinting in the moonlight, as if propelled by motors or wings, are gliding above the mounds of snow, getting further and further away from me. Then they are swallowed up into the thick darkness between the trees. I keep falling into snow up to my waist. My long hair is catching on branches. Large clumps are tearing out of my scalp. I am waiting to hear gunshots. Instead I hear a crack, a sound of a thin branch breaking.

That is when I see my baby tossed across a felled trunk. Her head is still attached to her body, but it is dangling. Her neck has been stretched into a long piece of something pink and rubbery. Like a giant piece of chewing gum. I pick up my baby, trying to wind the elongated stretch of pink flesh to keep her head from swinging. I keep thinking, if I can get back to the house fast enough, my husband will get Band Aids out of the grandparents' medicine cabinet in their bathroom. He will know how to attach our little girl's neck back to her head.

I am hovering over my sleeping husband, screaming, "Szyjke jej zlamali, szyjke jej zlamali," ..." He wakes up and yawns, mumbling, "What are you screaming about? Stop it! You'll wake up the baby!" He puts a pillow over his head, turns away from me and our broken baby and begins to snore.

At the moment when the state of sleeping and waking is not quite sorted out, I think, why doesn't he care that Nazis broke our baby's neck? Why are we sleeping in separate beds? Where am I?

Sunlight glinting from behind layers of window drapes coaxes me into the morning. Oh, yes, it does. I look toward the other twin bed and I remember.

My husband is no longer my husband. He is lying in a bed across from mine asleep, in a rose colored room in a hotel in Venice.

What, if anything, is he dreaming about? Is Matthew ever making visitations to comfort or disturb his nighttime hours?

Even though daylight has begun to invade the room, night and dream continued to cling to me. Some time passed before I felt fully awake thinking "enough of that!" and swung my legs over the side of the bed. My feet were reassured by the feel of the terry cloth square on the floor and the terry cloth mules placed on it each evening by the hotel maid when she comes to turn down the bed and leave a chocolate wrapped in a shiny wrapping on the pillow. I ignored the mules and pattered barefoot to the bathroom.

Serious spraying and scrubbing were needed to cleanse the layers of the night. Gradually the cascade of water from the two rotating showerheads chased away the nocturnal fog. I washed my hair and pulled a comb and brush through it. There was a high tech dryer resting in its cradle next to the mirror, but it was noisy. The dripping wet hair clung to my neck and down my back and helped with the morning revival.

On the marble counters, all kinds of good smelling toiletries were lined up, waiting to be dipped into. I rubbed moisturizer into my cheeks and forehead. I doused myself with eau de cologne. I put on eye make-up and some pale lipstick. Of the face looking back at me from the mirror, I asked, "Does it matter?" There was no answer.

I slipped on a fluid white cotton dress sprinkled with little flowers, stepped into very comfortable espadrilles, picked up my wide brimmed straw hat and hurried out. I drank my coffee and sambucca con la mosca in the usual shaded corner of the terrace. I was determined to take care of the first class return tickets.

Exiting the Alitalia office on San Marco, I heard a voice behind me, "Well, hello! There you are! He let you out again."

I stood face to face with the drunk from Harry's Bar.

"As you see," I blurted out.

Sidling up to me with his gauche pick-up lines the day before, I had been sure the man was on "independent activity" leave from of one of those elder groups, whose obedient members, like herded sheep, follow a tour guide holding a stick with a piece of identifying bright cloth waving in the air. Not slumped on a barstool, morning fresh in the light of day, before me stood a tall man, not only well dressed, but expensively well dressed. Navy linen blazer, crisp white shirt, Windsor knotted striped silk tie in pastel shades, well pressed white trousers. He was wearing socks with his polished loafers this time. He carried a Ferragamo briefcase. Before me stood an elegant, not at all bad looking man of a certain age.

"Where are you off to?" he asked. "Would you care to join me for a coffee?"

I hesitated for only a second. I was curious. I couldn't pass up a chance to try to square the image and demeanor of this elegant man with the slobbering, boorish drunk from Harry's Bar.

"Actually, that would be nice," I said. "I haven't had my coffee yet," I lied.

The piazza was not yet crowded. Only one of the bands was tuning up. At the outdoor table of the nearest San Marco café, he held the chair for me.

"Henry Medford," he introduced himself with a slight bow before sitting down. "At your service."
Old fashioned charm and polish had replaced the crude slurs in Harry's Bar. It hardly mattered, but, at the spur of the moment, I introduced myself with a made up name. When we shook hands, I was taken aback by his grasp. I have always disliked limp handshakes.

Over our cups of steaming latte, Henry Medford and I fell into easy touristy small talk about the beauty of Venice. About how lovely it was to sit on the Piazza before all the crowds arrived. The encounter of the previous day was not mentioned. I was surprised that he had even remembered one of the remarks he had made at Harry's Bar.

And here we were, face to face, drinking coffee at a café on Piazza San Marco. I didn't want to come out with: "Where are you from? What do you do?' He must have anticipated such thoughts.

"I am a fundraiser," he said. "Our organization in Chicago is involved with the rescuing of Venice. Trying to keep it from sinking into the waters."

His background was in architecture and art history, he said. He had been meeting with local Italian civic groups in charge of stemming the erosions and rebuilding of the foundations of La Serenissima. Except for my being right about the Midwestern inflection in his speech, I continued to have a hard time reconciling this proper gentleman with the crude oaf of the previous encounter.

"And, you, what do....?" he began.

With a smile, acknowledging his drunken opening line at Harry's Bar, I nodded and interrupted his question,,

"I do paint," I said. "And I sometimes dabble in theatre."

He made a cute, clownish face that meant, See, I am clever.

"I don't really like to call myself an artist," I said. I didn't. "I make things, that's all." I added: "I live in New York City."

We continued maneuvering through art talk. About the Tiepolos and Tintorettos we both admired. About the patchy gaudiness of Saint Mark's Cathedral. About the two Palladio Churches.

"I have always loved San Giorgio Maggiore," I said.

On Piazza San Marco, the tourists had not yet invaded, but the pigeons whooshed and swooped. "It's hard to love pigeons," I said. "Though I do have respect for them. They are not fond of nature. These birds prefer architecture."

"Well, then," Henry Medford, quick on the uptake, laughed. A nice, rich laugh. "I am doing a good thing. I am saving buildings for them."

He was charming and civilized and obviously well heeled. I was sorry that my newfound respect for the gentleman could not shake the memory of his soggy attempts at the earlier seduction. And the fleeting contact with his hand moments earlier led me to further unpleasant thoughts of flesh touching flesh. Mister Medford unzipping his fly, dropping his well pressed trousers, burrowing into me, clamping rubbery lips onto a nipple.

I tried to wipe clean that thought by recalling the sweet beer breath of the Polish boy. And a recent ride on the back of his "hog." Speeding on the FDR at dawn, my arms wrapped around his middle, from under the helmet my hair whipping my face, I wasn't afraid, no! I was exhilarated. I was terrified....

"You mentioned you are not alone in Venice," Henry Medford went on to say. He seemed to remember so well what he had said in Harry's Bar the day before. Causing me to question if he had really been as drunk as he had pretended to be?

"Who is this phantom you say you are 'attached' to?" he asked now.

"Phantom" was not far from the truth. English, lovely, often treacherous, rich feast of a language. 'Specter,' 'Shade,' 'Shadow' of his former self. 'Spirit'…,'My soon to be dead'….,'Ghost'.

"I am here with my husband," I said. "He is dying of cancer."

"I am so sorry," said mister Henry Medford.

For what? For flirting? For presuming? For not guessing he was inviting a dying man's tipsy wife into some hotel bed? Or, for buying her a cup of Italian coffee? Henry's hand sprinkled with quite a few brown spots reached for mine.

Ignoring the outstretched hand, I stood up, "I do have to go."

"Yes, of course," Henry Medford sighed and looked at his watch. It was some weighty Swiss concoction. "And I must not be late for my meeting at *C'a Rezzonico*."

He took a card out of the breast pocket of his blazer. Handing it to me, he winked.

"One never knows," he said. Then added, "One can always hope."

Did Henry Medford need to be reminded that Pandora let all the illusions from her treasure chest scatter to the winds and, as a cosmic tease, left us "Hope?"

One knew.

"Thank you for the coffee and company," I said. Not extending my hand. "And I wish you great, good luck with helping to keep Venice afloat."

After taking a few quick steps I turned around. Our coffee cups and crumpled paper napkins were still left on the table. Henry Medford was gone.

My short walk back to the hotel gave me enough time to review *"l'affaire"* Henry Medford. Venice is not large. But, how convenient to "run into" the lady who popped in alone, at noon, to down a strong drink, that quickly became two, at the bar in Harry's Bar. He really may not have been as drunk as he had pretended to be. I had been a snooty tease at the bar. He might have guessed, I would be an easier seduction if he changed tactics. And, how clever, at a time when many Americans were contributing money to the propping up and restoration of crumbling Venice, to cloak himself in the worthy pose of a fundraiser. And what if he had spotted me with my husband on one of our strolls? Or at the sunlit table of the fegato restaurant? He would have had no trouble guessing the condition of the man by my side. He may even have tailed us to the hotel. Fundraiser? Background in architecture and art history? How much of an expert did one have to be to have a superficial tourist chat about the treasures of *La Serenissima*. My hanging around Venice with my dying, no longer husband. was creepy enough without having to watch out for a dragueur at our backs.

It was not yet noon when I got back to our rose colored hotel room. My husband was up. Showered and dressed.
"You have been out touristing again," he said.
I was about to tell him that I had gone to confirm the First Class seats on our return flight when I stopped myself. I had lied to him about having taken care of the tickets the day before. Would he have remembered? Should I treat my husband to a sanitized version of the drinks at Harry's Bar? I decided against that. But I couldn't resist saying;
"I ran into an interesting American man I met, at the Alitalia office." Remembering to add, "The other day. He invited me for coffee on the Piazza."
"Oh," said my husband. There was a pause. He must have realized the absurdity of further questioning.
In that instant, I thought: If I am right about Henry Medford, am I so different from him or his possible lying? I was keeping a secret about the flirtation in Harry's Bar. About skipping out on "the drunk," letting him pay for my drinks. About having coffee with the same drunk, now sober, on Piazza San Marco. Interesting man, indeed! Little scams, minor white lies .... bigger scams, major black lies,... Flattery,... deception,... cheating, ... falling sideways into perdition... Isn't it all collected in the same playbook?
I moved on. "There is a Matisse show at the *Museo Correr*."

I had noticed the posters for the exhibition the day before. The Museo was just a walk across to the other side of San Marco.
"Are you up for that?" I asked. "It's not far."
"I remember that museum," he said. "I know where it is."

My husband had always loved Matisse. When we were still in art school, when we had first been a couple, my vigorous and gifted boyfriend, whose attentions I had been so thrilled with and been so proud of, had painted me, his new girlfriend, his future wife seminude draped in a vivid striped shawl. A la Matisse.
"I don't want to waste the whole morning sleeping again," he said. "I feel good today."
He did seem stronger.
"It must have been last yesterday's liver," I suggested.
"Please, don't make me eat that again," he laughed. For a split second I thought my witty old beau was by my side.
We crossed the Piazza. Several cafe bands were tuning up, ready to start competing with each other and with the clinking of glasses and crockery and tourist merriment. Pigeons, always the pigeons, shitting on the columns and porticos and swooping and swirling between the tourists and their cameras and their offerings of crumbs from half eaten, left over panini and dolci.
We had to walk up one flight to the primo piano. I was about to ask if he could manage when he had

already grabbed hold of the railing and was climbing up the rather steep stairs.

Except that there was a fee to be paid to the receptionist at a desk by the entrance, there was nothing of a Venetian museo about the space. A painted white rectangular room, with well placed recessed lighting and windows with translucent paper shades could have been a gallery in Soho, New York. There were no other visitors. We had the place to ourselves.

My husband's pitiful, thin body and sallow blemished face covered with cake makeup contrasted with painting after painting of lushness in the Matisse portraits of reclining, languid odalisques that exuded life's breath and ease in sunlit rooms and gardens.

One painting, larger than the others, stood apart from the portraits and draped nudes. A woman in black sits rigidly in a chair. Opposite her, a man in blue striped pajamas fills the space with his straight, angular figure. The lower edge of the canvas cuts him of at the knees. The upper edge lops of the top of his head. Against a deep blue wall, divided by a filigreed railing, the two figures facing each other are painted as flat cut-outs. Outside of the window frame, Matisse-like flora, flat greens, dotted with splashy redish pinks, suggest an overgrown garden. At first glance the figures of both man and woman suggest a moment of placid contentment. A closer contemplation at the angular placement of the two figures, facing each other, leads the viewer to suspect that something is not all that calm and peaceful in this domestic scene.

"Doesn't this painting make you think of us?" my husband turned to me saying.

The painting may elicit that obvious thought in many couples. The sick and dying man by my side made me feel as if he had delivered a slap across my face, making me want to shake his frail body and scream:

You and I can wander around Venice until you collapse or, until I drown in sambucca or vino bianco or cognac, or San Giorgio Maggiore and all of the treasures of Venice sink into the lagoon and float out to the Adriatic, but there will never again be "us!"

"Matisse was the best," said my husband, continuing his careful slow pace around the gallery. "The best."

SHARDS

1.

He was turned to the rose colored wall, deeply asleep. Again. As he had been on every one of our Venice mornings. What, if anything, did he dream about? Was Matthew ever making visitations to comfort or disturb his nighttime hours?

I was up and done with my ablutions, ready to head for the terrazzo for my morning coffee with sambucca con mosca. And church.

On this, our one and only Sunday in Venice, I wanted to go to Mass.

On the other side of the Doge's Palazzo, I entered the Gothic church of San Zaccaria, dipped my right hand in the Baptismal fount, bowed and crossed myself. The organ chords sounded. Mass was just starting. To avoid being an obstacle to those getting up later to take communion, I found a seat at the end of an empty mid-aisle. The presiding young priest, flanked by two altar boys bowed and began the *"Kyrie Eleison, Christe Eleison."* The ancient Greek words from the liturgy of long ago flowed into the post ecumenical contemporary words of the Mass in Italian.

At the early morning mass in San Zaccaria, the congregation consisted of a sparse group of elderly people, mostly women with black scarves covering their heads and a few bare headed men, holding their hats on their laps.

Niania had made me into a little Catholic girl, who loved the mass in Latin. She taught me how to say the Rosary and hung medals of the Holy Mother and the Christ Child and Saints around my neck. She assured me the benevolent Holy Mother and the Sacred Heart would protect me. I so wanted to go to the altar with all the other people attending mass, and kneel before the priest, and come away with my hands clasped and the taste of the pale wisp of the wafer placed on my tongue. Niania wouldn't allow it. Not then. When the Nazis were gone I would be baptized, she promised me. And she would get me a beautiful white dress and a wreath of lilies and roses to wear on my head for my first communion. I did have my own pearly white rosary. But, until I was properly baptized, I was forbidden to partake of the body of Christ. And I obeyed Niania still.

Much as I often wallowed in the pleasures of knowing the English language, within the new Latin deprived Mass, "The Lord be with You," and the response: "And also with you," had been shorn of its mystery. In Italian, *"Il Signore sia con te,"* and, *"E anche con te,"* came closer to the Latin. I still missed the severe resonance and mystery of *"Dominus Vobiscum"* and *"Ed cum Spiritum Tuum"* I had loved as a child.

I followed the words and music in the Italian hymnal. I joined in the responses and the singing. The organ music and the voices around me led the way. I followed the words and music in the Italian Hymnal. For all that, whatever language of the liturgy I may be musing on, in church I was not only just a visitor, but a pretender, taking a triumphant pleasure in knowing that unlike that Christmas morning in 1944, I would not be found out. I would not be booted out. I would leave the church along with the elderly Italian Catholics and be sad. But I would be safe.

My mind began to wander. I looked toward the arches at the side chapel to my right, making me think of the semicircular curve of the large window in the Park Slope house. Within a deep recess there glowed a restored Bellini altarpiece. The painted trompe l'oeil arch bordering the painting of the Madonna steadying a wise looking naked baby Christ balanced on her knee, echoed the marble arch of the chapel. The Holy mother and the child flanked by an elegant, formally arranged, contemplative grouping of Saint Lucie, Saint Catherine, Saint Thomas and a laic figure, probably depicting the rich donor. In the foreground, an angelic musician is poised to play an ancient viol.

At the completion of the mass, on the way out, I stopped to drop coins into the slot of the wooden box placed before the ubiquitous stand of slender tapers. Many were lit, creating levels in a forest of flickering flames. I lit one, and a second anchoring the candles into the spiky protrusions that would keep the candle upright until it dripped, burned down and died. I smiled at the thought of my husband's past reactions to my Church candle offerings for the departed.

"I understand the impulse to do it for your nanny," he had teased me. "But when you do it for your parents, they must be turning in their graves."

I watched the men exiting church, putting their summer hats back on. In the balmy air of a summer Sunday morning in Venice, my thoughts turned back to one cold and windy January evening on a street corner on the Upper West Side of Manhattan.

My husband and I had been trying to say goodbye to my father after we had gone with him to visit my mother in the hospital. At seventy her womb had slipped. With some current medical nips and tucks it had been coaxed back. She was recuperating well and would be allowed to leave the hospital within days. I was impatient for us to be on our way.

"I tel yu somesing!" my father turned to my husband. "Vy yu not vear aa hat?" And, he did not mean a warm knit cap. He meant a proper gentleman's hat, like the homburg he wore. With lifted forefinger of a gloved hand, he underscored the wisdom of the elder; "Yu shoult veaar aa hat!"

"I don't like wearing hats," his son-in-law answered. "You know that."

My husband was patient. He had learned to live with the constant, "I tell yu somesing," and "yu shoult" commandments. I threw a pleading look at him. He may have settled into a weary acceptance of the posturing of his Easter European in-laws. As well as with my constant impatience. I tugged at the sleeve of his leather jacket.

"We are already late," I murmured.

Moments earlier, propped up on pillows in her hospital bed, my mother had started her variation of "vy yu don't." Her attention was focused on my hair. "Vy yu don't poot up you' haair?" She also objected to the recent, discreet blond streaks the hairdresser had added.

"I am married to a man who likes my hair long and flowing." I turned to my husband, reminding her that I had a pillar to lean on. "And streaked with highlights. "

He treated my mother to an emphatic nodding of his head. And me to a reassuring smile, that meant: Why are you still surprised? Or, don't lose your sense of humor. He knew well that in the presence of my parents my "sense of humor" turned to a dark shade of night.

Time to go. To get away from the distasteful pictures I had in my head of my mother's legs spread out, anchored in the stirrups and the doctor entering her vagina, barreling through to rearrange her no longer useful femaleness.

When the moment came to plant the quick obligatory exit kiss on my mother's cheek, I held my breath. The smell of hospital and age and her excessive use of voda colonska wafted toward me.

"Ze doctor tolt me," my father prattled away, "Yu haf ze helsiest voman heerr!"

On the cold street, after we had said our good-byes, at last, my husband and I watched the slight receding figure of my father, clutching his briefcase, bending against the wind, heading to the nearest subway stop. I caught a last glimpse of the homburg disappearing down into the "subvey."

"Maybe we should have asked him to come with us," my husband said.

"You know how that would play," I sighed.

"Yes, I know," he agreed.

We both knew. We had tried the restaurant scenario "en famille." Even when we had gone to a

Viennese restaurant that had "Wiener schnitzel" on the menu, my father, when his plate arrived, would sniff at it, maybe even try a morsel or two. It would not have tasted the way he remembered it from a long time ago in Vienna or Kraków. And he would let the waiter know; "I tell yu somesing...."

My husband and I walked into the nice French restaurant on Manhattan's East Side. It was lively and full. Our friends were already seated at a banquette. I was more than ready to dive into food and drink and smart chit-chat, sprinkled with bon mots and smart phrases in proper English. But underneath the easy interlude of good food and drink and the deserved sense of wellbeing, I could not erase the image of the small bent figure, disappearing into the underworld of the city subway to an empty apartment in Rego Park.

The following spring, after retiring from his job at the cosmetic factory, my father had a massive stroke. After lingering for a week hooked up to a feeding tube through his nose and a catheter leading to a urine bag dangling at the side of the hospital bed he was dead.

Until she ended up in a nursing home, my father's "helsy voman," alone in her Rego Park apartment, outlived him by several years. During my obligatory visits, even though her mind no longer was able to obey the rules of continuous thought, she still managed to rewind the tapes recorded in her brain that played the comments about my hair.

Then, she would turn her attention to the vase on the table by her bed to scold me, because when I walked into the room, I had interrupted her conversation in Polish with her other visitors, her flowers.

My parents were gone. Buried side by side, in burials so many years apart, in a Jewish cemetery in New Jersey. Their funerals had been prepaid for and arranged by the Jewish Friends Society they had joined when we came to America.

2.

Returning to the hotel room I was once again surprised by my husband out of bed and dressed and leftover breakfast dishes on the little table.

"I went to church," I told him.

"Did you light candles?" he asked smiling.

"I certainly did," I said. I was reassured by the rolling of his eyes in the old, anticipated way.

I headed for the bathroom to pee, to splash water on my face.

"Let's go for a walk," I suggested when I came out. I didn't feel like lingering in our messy rose-colored room. "Are you up for it?" He hesitated, but didn't say "no."

"I need to change my shirt," he said.

He had only just dressed, yet blotches of sweat were already visible on his shirt.

I took a fresh white shirt from the hanger in the armoire and handed it to him. He had trouble inserting his arms into the sleeves. I watched his thin, trembling fingers fumble with the buttons and buttonholes. When he unzipped his fly and began tucking the shirt into his pants, he looked at me, pointed to his crotch, "This doesn't work anymore," he said. I turned away.

God, I was ready to be done with this Venice trip!

Leaving the hotel, we walked into the heat and cloying pomeriggio air drifting in from the Canale Grande. We found a cooler dark calle that led in the direction away from the pigeons and the tourists and the operetta music of San Marco.

On Campo Santo Stefano, the massive church cast a shadow on a substantial part of the little square. My husband nodded toward the façade where a gelato vendor leaned, half dozing, against a column.

"Would you like one?" I asked. He nodded and said "yes." I was always glad to hear him express interest in something to eat.

Watching the vendor fill the waffled cone with one generous scoop of vanilla and adding another of pistachio did make my mouth water. Their watercolor translucence so different from the more opaque, denser, milkier American ice creams. With all the vino, cognac, sambucca, I was saving my caloric intake for, I denied myself the sweet Italian delicacy.

I smiled at the vendor, paid him "Grazie, Signore, and placed the filled cone in my husband's hand. Once again, taking note of how very thin his fingers had become.

We walked a few steps toward the ornate cistern in the center of the square which I recognized from that last, happy time we had come to Venice. When we had been surprised and amused by the many roaming local cats that seemed to have made the area into their regular hangout. We had soon discovered why. Black clad ladies came here to empty their pots and pans of leftovers. That must have been a daily routine. And the cats knew it.

We had been delighted to watch the Venetian street felines fight over and pounce on generous scraps of meat and fish and pasta. It was the first time we had seen cats gorge on spaghetti with tomato sauce.

These feral animals would never know that their American relatives ate special canned and boxed foods. And they were taken to doctors in well designed carrying cases to be injected with shots to protect them from diseases and to be operated on to protect them from the dangers of normal cat pleasures.

"We take these wild, lusty creatures and make stuffed pillows out of them," my husband used to quip.

I watched him taking small licks from the top of his double gelato.

"Let's sit down," I said. We moved toward a nearby iron bench. He was about to ease himself into a seating position when I saw the cone in his hand crack, break in half and crumble, causing gelato scoops to plop onto the ground.

"Oh, no," I cried. "How did that happen?"

My husband didn't move. He stood there, bent over, as gobs of the pale green and yellowish remnants of ice cream dripped and melted between his fingers. He held the remaining part of the emptied cone in his outstretched hand, like a beggar waiting for a coin to be dropped into his paper cup.

Had there been a neural tremor causing his fingers to loosen their grip? What if it had been a spasm that would lead to a stroke. "Are you….?" I began.....

"I'm alright," he snapped. He continued to stare at the melting gelato drips spreading on the ground at his feet.

I dipped my handkerchief in the dripping water of the cistern and handed it to him.

Tossing the leftover piece of broken cone he stamped it into the cobblestone ground, wiped his sticky hands and handed the messy handkerchief back to me.

"It is for me," he said, his raspy voice seething with anger.

"Your pacifying me with me another Italian gelato isn't going to change that."

3.

After almost a week of hanging around Venice, by the side of this wreck of a man, with the spilled gelato melting at his feet, I wanted to be done with "nice and grand" and "taking care of papa." Right there and then, I wanted to take him back to the hotel, pack up his traveling bag, load him onto a water taxi heading to the airport, and put him on an Alitalia flight back to New York. His paid companion or one of his coterie of small men or his children could "take care of papa" when he arrived back home.

And I would wave "arrivederci Venezia," and hop on a plane and fly off to Paris. Or, Stockholm. And stay under the radar for a good chunk of time.

Of course, I was not about to do any such thing. But I did get angry.

"I didn't knock the gelato cone out of your hand," I snapped at him. "You are still here..... And the gelato man, still standing right over there, would welcome another sale!"

He continued to sulk. The Italian ice cream cone had betrayed him. His body had betrayed him. He had betrayed him. And I rewound back to pity and sadness for this dejected man, sitting there, folding, caving into himself.

I imagined how, at another time in his, in our life, he would have found the giggle in this minor mishap. How it might have inspired a funny story and a picture of a sad anthropomorphic mouse, or cat, or pig, in proper human attire, crying big drops of graphic tears for the loss of a sock, or a moon disappearing from view behind a cloud, or dropped scoops of melting ice cream.

I wished the stray cats would reappear. And, with their little sandpapery tongues lick the ground clean of gelato puddles.

He would have gladly sacrificed his wasted treat to them.

But the cats and the women in black never showed. The food distribution ritual must have moved on to another campo.

We sat side by side on a wrought iron bench on Campo Santo Stefano on a hot summer afternoon in Venice, not having much to say to each other.

After a while we began a slow, very slow, walk back to our hotel. As soon as we got to the room he eased himself onto the bed and letting out a deep sigh, sank his head against the plump pillows in their linen and lace cases. He seemed completely spent. I was still not certain that a serious tremor in his hand hadn't been the cause of the spilled gelato. I wanted to get some food into him.

"If I call for room service," I ventured to ask. "Will you eat something?" He shrugged. Then nodded "yes."

It was too early for dinner. Too late for tea? Too late for everything, I thought and reached for the phone.

A large tray of panini and aqua minerale and strawberries was brought and set on the coffee table in front of the brocaded settee. The little sandwiches came garnished with baby watercress. Small wild straw berries were heaped on a bed of mint leaves in a woven basket. There was fresh cream in an ornate round pitcher. There were crystal glasses and linen napkins. There was a bud vase with two miniature yellow roses. Yellow roses! Perfect. For this mockery of l'amour l'après midi. All that was needed was the split of Veuve Clicquot, I knew nestled in the mini bar.

My tired, sick husband did sit up and take a few bites of a prosciutto filled panino. Then, all at once, he was up and headed for the bathroom.

Now what? I thought. An attack of vomiting?

Would I have to clean up after him? Or embarrass myself by calling someone from the hotel staff to do it?

No sounds of retching came from the bathroom. Only the whoosh of the toilet and the noise of water splashing in the sink. I was relieved to see him come out wearing pajamas and looking refreshed.

"Better?" I asked in the voice of a professional caretaker. Knowing well that there was no "better" for him. Better had vanished... was continuing to vanish with each passing moment.

"You should try to take a few more bites of your sandwich," I cajoled.

"I am not hungry," he said reaching for his medicine pouch. I poured him a glass of the minerale and watched him swallow several pills.

"At least have a few of the strawberries," I tried. "After swallowing all those pills, they'll be tasty...and sweet...and clean your palette."

Jesus, I was turning into Nurse Ratchet, pretending to be Mary Poppins.

He ignored me, lay down on the bed, didn't even remove his glasses. Letting his head fall back onto the soft, lacy pillows, he closed his eyes and was soon asleep.

I watched his profile. It was beginning to look two dimensional. His nose pointing to the ceiling reminded me of the dead Benedictine nun whose body had been laid out in the convent chapel. It was the old nun I had spied on through a keyhole while she was taking a bath. I had never considered nuns having naked bodies, using soap and splashing in tubs of water. Sister's shrouded dead body, hands clasped around a rosary and crucifix on her chest, so still on the black draped catafalque, looked like the right nun thing to be.

Her thin sharp point of the nose was the closest to the chapel ceiling. The closest to Heaven, I remembered thinking then, the closest to the Holy mother and the Christ child. There were no thoughts of heaven connected to my husband's nose pointing straight up at the hotel room ceiling.

Not until I heard his regular breathing, interspersed with slight puffs of snoring sounds, did I open the door to the minibar. Ignoring the split of champagne in the mini refrigerator. I opened one of the little bottles of cognac and poured it into the snifter. Settling into one of the brocaded armchairs, I nibbled on a prosciutto filled panino. I soon followed the first cognac with a second. The wild strawberries and sweet cream were perfect. I finished the whole serving.

The Venetian air scented with flowers, mixed with the constant sweetish, rotten smells from the canals, wafted through the half opened window. The drapes stirred. The man stretched out on the bed did not. Most probably he would stay that way through the evening. Maybe even through the rest of the night.

I showered. I put on my white flower printed cotton dress. I slipped out into the balmy evening air of July in La Serenissima. I wasn't looking for adventure. I was hoping I was not right about Henry Medford tailing me, lurking behind a column or materializing from beneath a flock of swooping pigeons. I was getting away from keeping a vigil by a sleeping, dying man in the cloistered atmosphere of our hotel room.

On Piazza San Marco I found a table at Café Quadri. All around me tables were full of groups and couples, filling the evening with a never ceasing hum of party. I would have liked a sambucca, but thought it may be wiser to stay with what I had been drinking and ordered a cognac. The band was fiddling, sawing away on the score from "Summertime." I may well have been sitting in the same spot the camera had focused on Hepburn when she first attracted the attention of the gallant Rosanno Brazzi.

The summer that movie opened, one of those brutally unrelenting heat waves had wrapped New York City in an airless cocoon. My husband and I, newly married, had escaped our small Brooklyn apartment and taken the subway to one of the huge movie theatres on Times Square. Yes, we did go to see the just released "Summertime." My husband loved Hepburn. But what we really wanted was to find relief in air conditioning. After sitting through two consecutive screenings, hating to leave the comfort of the chilly movie house we could not bring ourselves to sit through a third showing of dear Katherine hanging out of the train window, waving farewell to the disappearing figure of Rosanno Brazzi and Venice.

Many years later, after my husband and I had been happy visitors in Venice, I watched the movie again. I came to look at the Katherine Hepburn heroine with a jaundiced eye. This woman wandering around Venice for a week, or ten days, pointing her tourist camera at this or that, dreaming of romance, saying hello and goodbye to everything she felt had eluded her, was not once seen entering a church or a museum. When I had arrived at that ungenerous thought, I found, the smiling through tears, romantic, aging heroine inane.

At that moment my hand hit my nearly empty glass of cognac. Remaining drops spilled on the tablecloth and the glass crashed to the ground and shattered. A cameriere was at my side in an instant. I made apologetic noises....

"*Fa niente, signorina,*" said the young handsome *cameriere*. "*Non e importa.*"

He called me "*signorina.*" How nice! I thought. And, how sad! That I had the need for such reassurance.

The shards of broken glass were quickly swept up. The stained tablecloth was replaced with a fresh one and a new glass of cognac was put before me.

On Piazza San Marco at Café Quadri, with no Rossano Brazzi, or even Henry Medford, to stalk and annoy me, I was sitting alone sipping my second, my replacement cognac, recalling the much more shattering moment years ago, at the kitchenette table in a fourth floor walk-up apartment in Brooklyn, when a small attachment to an ordinary kitchen vessel ruined the simple pleasure of sipping coffee out of a coveted cup of antique French crockery.

HALLOWEEN PARADE

1.

He had been sick for two of the three and a half years we had lived apart. Since our return from Venice my husband's condition had been deteriorating at a steady pace. Once, a high fever led to an overnight hospital stay. A few weeks after that, Jerry was called to a sudden audition, leaving the sick man alone for several hours. He fell that afternoon, banging his head against a sharp table corner. That led to several stitches above his right eye. Which led the children to want to fire Jerry.

"Well, then, it will be up to you two to find a replacement," I said. Not in the mood for a family negotiation, I was turning to stone. "And do it fast."

That did it. Jerry stayed. The righteous kids calmed down. Their father's gash healed. The stitches were taken out. It didn't matter. The remaining scar was only a minor addition to the many other blemishes on his face. About those nothing could be done. My husband and I continued to talk on the phone, not daily, but often enough. He was the one to call first. I was busy at my desk, staying away from the Washington Square apartment as much as I could.

One day in mid October I got a call. He was making plans. "I would like to walk in the Village Halloween parade," he announced. "In my gorilla suit."

I waited for what I knew was coming next.

"On the street,... in such a crowd," he said, "It'll be hard for me to see out of the little eye slits in the gorilla head." There was a slight pause. "Could you come with me?" he asked. "As my guide?"

I had never made a secret of how I felt about Halloween, and he could well guess that, in the current atmosphere, I would have no desire to have anything to do with the West Village Saint Vitus dance. The Venice trip had pretty much cured me of further volunteering of "helpful" and "nice."

"Why don't you ask Jerry?" I snapped. "He'll be thrilled by the attention he'd get guiding King Kong up Sixth Avenue!" We left it at that. I left it at that. And climbed back into my shelter of contempt for all things Halloween. And more.

The remembrance of my Catholic past, prevented me from thinking about the last day of October and the first day of November as anything but days of mourning. A time for attending Solemn Mass and visiting graves with bouquets of chrysanthemums. The Halloween hoopla I was introduced to when I came to New York, with kids and grown-ups decking themselves out as pirates and skeletons and devils, I considered not only idiotic, but sacrilegious.

When our children were young, and I found myself in the midst of the yearly "what are you going to be for Halloween?' echoing and circulating ad nauseum, among them and their friends. Not wanting to poison their contemporary theatrics with my wartime European residues, I put my dislike on hold. I baked cookies and bought candy and collected pennies and dimes to distribute. My husband and I helped with costumes for our two Halloweeners.

When they no longer lived at home, whatever Halloween parties or get-ups they were playing with in their away places, we would get to see only in photographs. I was free to revert to my dislike and ignore Halloween. In our darkened house, peeking from behind a window curtain to watch hopeful trick-or-treaters climb the stone steps to the front door and ring the doorbell to a house where, I, the ghoul, often alone in the dark, lurked behind the door that stayed shut.

The gorilla suit my husband wanted to climb into for the current Halloween parade had been a present from our daughter one Christmas several years before the final dissolution of our marriage. During her stay in LA, working backstage at Universal Studios, she had learned how to use a variety of materials to build theatrical costumes. She had built the gorilla from a glossy black imitation fur with a molded elastic breast plate and equipped it with an industrial zipper in the back to make it easy to step into. She had completed the costume with a sculpted head, which slipped on like an old diving helmet. Heavy black gloves with tufts of the fur-like material and knitted feet with separate toes completed the costume.

When her stunned father opened the huge box and gasped with delight and admiration, she said: "Papa, except for the gorilla head, it's just like the pajamas with feet I used to like so much when I was little."

We helped to zip him into the body of the suit and slip on the head. He lumbered and grunted and pounded his breastplate until he got too hot. Which didn't take long. It was the best present to be opened that Christmas morning. And the best entertainment at our yearly, big drunken Christmas party that followed in the late afternoon and evening.

2.

All Hallow's Eve arrived. At my drawing desk by an open window, I was working on a picture of an elaborate portal flanked by Corinthian columns leading to a castle in the fairy tale I was illustrating.

I could hear the muffled hoots and shrieks and music from the parade participants and the crowds of onlookers funneling through the side streets, to get closer to those who were already lining 6th Avenue. I intended to stay put. There had been no further communication from my husband about his gorilla appearance for Halloween.

As if it knew I was really itching to get away to find out if a black ape was over there, somewhere, participating in the parade, the drawing refused to obey the scratch of my tiny pen nib and swish of paintbrush. I was curious and I was nervous. Maybe I shouldn't have been so hasty? Maybe I should have gone with him after all. I put down pen and brush, covered the unfinished, uncooperative illustration with a piece of tracing paper, turned off the work lamp, grabbed a pair of opera glasses and a jacket and walked out.

It was one of those still warm evenings, when autumn in New York City was held back by a last embrace of summer. The color in the sky had turned into a smooth, deep, airbrushed cobalt with a dab of Prussian I liked to call "Manhattan Blue."

The side streets were crowded. I pushed my way through the throng until I found a spot near the 4th street subway entrance, somewhat behind people lining the front part of the barrier erected between the onlookers and the marchers. Ghosts are invisible, I mused. I intended to be a ghost.

At first it was difficult to focus on much in the general melee of bodies moving, twirling in vibrating colors and theatrical contortions, grimacing faces and much cacophony.

Through my opera glasses the first marchers I zoomed in on was a chorus line of buxom drag queens poured into spectacular sequined showgirl gowns. On their heads towered wigs of platinum, lime green, Pepto-Bismol pink and Windex blue. They were kicking up their legs, executing a well rehearsed imitation of the Rockettes. There followed an impressive quartet of black clad puppeteers, manipulating dowels with rattling skeletons swooping back and forth, between the marchers like fluttering butterflies. Then came some Paper Bag players with dopey expressions painted on their elongated brown bag faces, which reached all the way down to their feet. Four horned red devils carried a giant papier-mache construction of the head of a reptilian monster. In its open maw, a group of children, [or, were they dwarfs?] with grimacing faces, were packed close together behind the fence of pointy teeth. I recognized this scary depiction of "The Mouth of Hell" from books of medieval illuminated manuscripts.

Right behind the "Mouth of Hell" float, with slow, measured steps, walked two angels in flowing white robes with giant spread wings. They held each other so close they might have been conjoined Siamese twins. One of the angels had wrapped a white kerchief around his head. The other had left his balding head with remaining tufts of hair uncovered. They had attached golden halos on trembling wires to narrow headbands. The two angels wore no make-up or masks. As if challenging certain death coming to better see them, in their free hands, the pair carried powerful flashlights to shine beams on the mass of lesions and blemishes mushrooming all over their faces.

When they passed by, the applause and whistles and stadium hoots went silent. To be replaced with chants of "Silence/Death! Silence/Death!" repeated here and there among the onlookers in the crowd.

At that moment, I was shoved aside by an aggressive, beefy, bearded guy in a leather motorcycle jacket and a heavy chain rattling from his belt. He was pushing through the throng of onlookers, followed by his tough looking girlfriend with badly bleached, spikey blond hair and a lot of make-up. From under her short denim skirt protruded fleshy bare legs in worn out Tony Lama cowboy boots

"Fucking faggots! "I heard the biker's raspy voice snarling. "This whole goddamn, shitty Halloween parade is nothing but faggots showing of!"

Continuing to swear and spit out obscenities, the guy and his doll elbowed their way through the crowd.

Their exit opened a spot for me to move closer to the marchers.

It was then I spotted the gorilla in the very center of the parade.

He was led by a thin chain held in the hand of a man in a circus tamer's costume. Tight pants, striped tee-shirt, an embroidered, glittering vest and top hat. It took me a second or two to recognize Jerry! And it soon became obvious that for the man in the gorilla suit each step was a major effort. He was bent over, focusing on the ground, making no attempt to look up or turn from side to side. If he emitted grunts or growls I would not have been able to hear them through all the parade noise. The slow halting pace set by this Kong worked to Jerry's advantage. Bowing and waving to the crowd, right and left, wielding a thin whip he oversaw his furry charge, all the while savoring the attention and applause of the crowd. My husband had been determined to take part in this spectacle but Jerry was the one who claimed it as his own showcase.

I remembered the year our nine-year old son, devoted to classic monster movies, an interest shared with his father, wanted to be the "Mummy" for Halloween. I tore a white sheet into long strips. While our boy turned and turned, his parents wrapped him in layers of the fabric strips. Only leaving openings for eyes and mouth. I painted a gold squiggle, that was supposed resemble a hieroglyph, on a black paper bag for collecting treats. Step by measured step, he went down the stairs and shuffled along the street with his arms extended before him in the manner of a sleepwalker or a walking dead. My husband not in costume, but with his arms crossed on his chest Egyptian mummy style, had followed a step or two behind.

I had been busy at our door distributing treats into greedy little hands holding up paper bags or plastic pumpkins when I glanced down the street to be surprised by the sight of father and son returning. Oh, dear, dear! I could see that our carefully swaddled mummy was unraveling. Strips of white sheet were trailing around our boy and sliding off his head and face. Even at a distance, I could tell he was miserable.

My husband told me later how the boy had pleaded, "Papa, please, fix me!" and how he had tried to tuck the strips of mummy shroud back in place. It didn't matter that many people who came to the doors thought that the unraveling was intentional, and that his treat bag was filling with a substantial haul of candy and cookies and pennies, the boy was crushed. No amount of reassurance could convince him that his costume hadn't been a complete failure for Halloween.

I wondered if these many years later the boy's father was experiencing a similar failure? Encased in his gorilla suit, weak and spent and probably sweating, in spite of the roars and applause from the crowd, did he feel that he was failing to deliver a good gorilla performance?

Through my opera glasses, until they were obscured by the next group of marchers, in my spot behind the barrier, anonymous, I continued my spying on the stumbling gorilla and his confident, strutting tamer. Then I pushed my way through the crowd and left the throng of parade watchers.

I walked toward Washington Square Park and planted myself in a doorway across the street from my husband's apartment building. I didn't have to wait long before I saw the now bareheaded man in the gorilla suit, leaning heavily on Jerry's shoulder, teetering, stumbling down the street. The circus tamer had reverted to his role as servant/nurse. He carried the gorilla head and his own top hat in the crook of his free arm. I watched them maneuver toward the door of the apartment building where they were met by the helpful doorman.

I left my hiding spot and walked back home. Back to my drawing desk. Back to trying to coax my uncooperative picture into behaving. If all this grotesque Halloween foolishness were to lead to his next attack, I would find out soon enough.

"…..YET IT WILL COME"

1.

That afternoon in murky, early December, I had forced myself to visit him during his latest stay in the hospital.

In bed in a private room, he was propped up against two pillows looking even more emaciated and sallow than the last time I had seen him at home. I did not think it possible for any more lesions to sprout on his face and arms. Nevertheless, new ones had found a way.

Out of a paper bag, I took a small carton of pistachio ice cream and handed it to him along with a plastic spoon. With a trembling hand, he brought the first spoonful to his chapped, grayish lips. All his gestures seemed to be happening in slow motion. By the time he finished slurping and the spoon was scraping against the bottom of the empty little container, the ice cream was well on the way to melting and dripping.

Only a few months had passed since that sad little incident on a Venetian piazza, when a gelato filled cone I had cracked, slipped out of his hand and tumbled onto the cobblestones. There, in the blazing sunlight of Venetian summer, he was frail and tired and furious at the Fates who were propelling him in only one direction. In spite of that, he had still belonged to the living. In this pinkish gray hospital room, with the green drapes partly drawn around the bed, the disease had gathered force, worming itself onto the surface and deeper into the body of the man who used to be my husband.

He handed me the empty carton and the spoon and patted his mouth with the paper napkin. "Thank you," he said, and treated me to a childish smile. "That was tasty."

Lying back against the hospital pillow he closed his eyes. He was very still. If he drops off to sleep right away, I thought, I won't stay.

A nurse came in. He was wearing jeans and a green hospital smock over a long sleeved gray tee shirt. His nametag let us know that he was Ricardo. The first time I had ever heard a young man declare a wish to become a nurse was in a comedy sketch by Nichols and May during the late sixties. Along with the rest of their followers and fans, my husband and I had laughed at the absurdity of such an idea. That was then.

"Are we up for a stroll?" nurse Ricardo asked the patient. Without waiting for a response, he turned to me and said: "He should try to get out of bed and move his legs."

"Of course," I said. "I will walk with him."

Since he had been diagnosed, when going with him to the hospital, I could not avoid medical personnel of various ranks asking me if the stricken man was my brother or my cousin. Even though after almost three years of my presence during these admissions and releases. I had become used to such questions, I still couldn't avoid bracing myself for them.

Ricardo wasted no time asking useless questions. He helped my husband to a sitting position, swung his legs over the side of the bed, pulled thick, red hospital ankle socks with those no-slip rubberized patterns onto his bony feet, and coaxed his patient to a standing position. From the forefinger of the sick man's right hand he detached the plastic clamp, which connected a cord to the heartbeat monitor and curved his frail hand around the pole with the IV drip bag.

"Just a short back and forth in the hallway," Ricardo said to me. "It's good for him."

What was "good for him," I wanted to tell nurse Ricardo, but didn't, this man had squandered at a deliberate pace over a long period of time.

Side by side, my husband and I began a very slow, measured walk along the silent, empty hospital corridor. He wasn't exactly wobbling, but I did hold on lightly to his left elbow. His right hand, holding fast to the rolling IV pole, kept him steadied.

"Lively place, isn't it," he smirked.

I was surprised by the vestige of wit I had so delighted in during our years together, still surfacing from this hollowed out man.

While he kept up a cautious but determined shuffle forward, to better observe his ambulating, I fell a half a step behind him. A telltale yellow stain had spread on the pale blue checkered hospital gown. The pistachio ice cream had not stayed in his entrails for long. The strings of the hospital gown had come untied in the back, just enough to expose the blotches of purple lesions on his thin buttocks.

I wasn't really sure that a smell was emanating from him, but the thought was enough to make me gag. I reached for a handkerchief in my pants pocket and held it to my nose and mouth.

Why was I putting one foot in front of the other in this ghastly hospital corridor by the side of this pitiful remnant of a man, whose years of cheating and hiding and unsavory secrets had brought him to this moment? Why, even after our Venice trip, during which I had plenty of time to see-saw on doubts and regrets, was I still clinging to this continuing, self imposed obligation? Was it a last gasp of an attempt to inject some goodness and purify the badness of our life together? Make of it some kind of a neat, virtuous package tied with a ribbon? Like the love letters we had written to each other when we were new and nice.

During the latest hospital stays, his daughter hardly visited at all.

"I can't do it," she said. "I can't watch him fading away, like your poor little gray cat did."

She was wrong about the cat. He didn't linger and do a slow fade. He knew when the time to go had come.

Our son, always hopeful, was planning to drop in to see his father the next day.

"If they let him go home, Mama," he said. "I'll be there to help"

Even though there were times when some kind of defiance produced in the sick man enough strength to hold on to a hope that the disease was not going to let the curtain fall, after all, I was weary with holding on to the pretense that plans should continue to be made for even the following day.

Our once so important family holiday would be upon us in less than three weeks. The children and I, facing a Christmas that most likely would be his last, had begun to talk about a small tree, some simple food and little token gifts.

The year before a Christmas Day get together with the children, Jerry, a couple of friends had almost succeeded. My son's fiancée and I had cooked. The table was set. We believed we had fooled the evil spirits once again. It was not to be. He collapsed and had to be rushed to the hospital with fever and tremors.

For the moment it was time to end the slow crawl through the hospital corridor when the sick man came to a sudden halt, almost causing the pole and the IV to tumble to the floor. I grabbed it just in time.

He turned toward me with a secretive grin on his face. "They put on shows here, you know," he said.

"What are you talking about?" I was unnerved. "Who puts on shows?"

"I am not sure if I am supposed to tell," he took his voice down into a raspy stage whisper.

"Today two Broadway gypsy dancers, dressed like doctors, leapt into my room and did a tap routine." My husband looked around, as if to make sure there was no one listening, before he went on.

"Then Ethel Waters came in to take away my bedpan," he said. "She sat down at the foot of my bed and sang, "His Eye is on the Sparrow" to me.

Moments earlier, the "lively place, isn't it?" remark had surprised me with a quiet burst of his former wit. That meant he was still all there. But, hallucinating theatrical performances from his past was not promising. Were we heading into the next phase of his downward slide?

He started to giggle. That led to a fit of coughing. Followed by hiccups. An older heavyset, black female nurse in one of those absurd, cheerful patterned smocks came toward us. Was she the singing Ethel Waters from the private performance he thought he had witnessed?

The nurse and I, together, guided my now unsteady husband and his rolling IV pole back to his room. We helped him get into bed. His thin body was convulsing to the rhythm of the hiccups. Out of a pitcher on the side table, the nurse poured water into a plastic cup and helped him hold it. He took a few sips through a straw, then sank back against the pillows. The hiccups continued. The nurse put an oxygen mask over his nose. She slipped the heart monitor clamp onto the forefinger of his right hand. The bleeps on the screen were erratic.

The nurse left and came back with a hypodermic needle. She pulled aside his hospital gown and sank an efficient jab into his thin buttock. Before I turned away, and she rearranged the hospital gown and recovered him with the sheet and blanket, I was not spared a glimpse of my husband's shriveled purplish penis.

I thanked the tacit large nurse. She left the room. There were longer pauses between the hiccups. Until, at last, they subsided altogether.

I stood, rigid, between the bed with its partially drawn green curtains and the messy side table with an overturned box of tissues, an unused washcloth and towel, the water pitcher with ice cubes melting, a stack of plastic cups and a recent copy of The New Yorker, I doubted he had even glanced at.

At the foot of the bed, on the rolling hospital serving cart, I could smell the leftover, maybe even untouched, food under the plastic domes. No one had bothered to take it away. From the monitor dangling above eye level could be heard a slight hum or buzz. Will hook-ups to feeding and breathing tubes and catheters and diapers come next? How long will the regular pace continue its measured repetition on the monitor screen before it began it led to alpine leaps ending with an unrelenting, neat straight line?

The gray December sky, like a wet brush stroke on watercolor paper, was bleeding into late afternoon. I waited until I was sure that my husband's hiccups did not return and he had drifted off to sleep before I walked away.

That evening at dinner in a Japanese restaurant in my Soho neighborhood, a satisfying plate of sushi and the reassuring glow from a bottle of sake in the company of the unexpected arrival of the man who, as if by magic, appeared at my door at exactly the perfect moment to take me out of the glum residue of the afternoon's hospital visit.

After dinner, coming out of the warmth and glow of the restaurant, I felt buffered not only against the increasing chill of December, but well prepared to project myself into the next day's hospital visit in the promised company of my son.

But I was not prepared, not really, for the moment after I had kissed my surprising, much welcome visitor "goodbye" and watched the yellow of the cab he had stepped into disappear and blend into traffic around the corner to see my doorman waving a piece of paper in his hand, running toward me with a grim look on his face.

"Mr. Jerry called," he was saying. "I didn't know where to reach...."

Mr. Jerry,...oh, God,.. "It's all right, Mike...," I said. "I am here now."

I grabbed the slip of paper with the scribbled, "Call Mr. Jerry immediately," and rushed past the doorman.

Before I pressed the number of my floor in the elevator, before I put the key in the lock of the door to my apartment, before I reached for the phone and dialed the number, hoping Jerry was there, I was ready to hear what I already not only suspected, but knew.

"He is gone," Jerry said.

"I should have been there..." I let go of a sob.

Only a few hours earlier, I had been there. I had walked with him. I had brought him pistachio ice cream. I had smelled him. Why hadn't I stayed through the afternoon?

"I should have,.... "I was going to be..." I kept blubbering. "I was planning to visit him tomorrow again ..."

Why was I justifying myself to Jerry?

"When I walked into his room earlier this evening," Jerry went on, "His doctor and two nurses were hovering over him, and ...." His voice went lower. "One of them was adjusting the intravenous and the other...."

"Yes, yes," I was impatient. "I am sure that...," I started to say...I wasn't sure of anything. "They must have been increasing the morphine dose,..." I imagined the medical team was adding something to the drip, or giving him a shot...

"I think they were doing more," Jerry interrupted in a theatrical whisper, "I think they were helping him pass..."

Oh, God, Jerry! No doubt you were witnessing a conspiracy. The medical profession was taking life away from a dead man. Just as the theatrical profession was forever taking parts away from you!

As though he may have read my mind, there was a pause on the line. I was straining to be done with this phone call.

"I have called the funeral home," I heard Jerry say.

Right after my husband had been admitted to this last hospital stay, Jerry had made me furious by bringing up the name of a funeral home recommended by his contacts at GMHC. Only very few funeral homes accepted bodies dead from AIDS. I hadn't wanted to listen. I snapped at him. I told him he was being presumptuous and ghoulish. Yes, as he had been many times before, the very sick man had been deposited in a hospital bed once more. But he was still here, I had snapped at him. It was indecent, it was bad luck, to fast forward plans for the disposal of his dead body.

I should have told Jerry that I was grateful. I was. I said nothing.

And I thought: "The readiness is all."

After almost two years of attacks and reversals, medical half promises beckoning, luring with the temptation of absurd hopes, he was no more. The man who used to be my husband was discontinued. Breath and thought and pain and desire were canceled. Shitting and pissing and manipulating and deceiving and the crafting of charming pictures and words had been terminated. What was left of his flesh and bone and brain would be shoved into temporary storage in a stainless steel drawer, far down in the refrigerated bowels of a massive concrete building seventy streets away from where I stood, clutching a phone receiver in my hand, waiting for facts to invade me, to envelop me, to kick me. I wondered if the sheet from the dead body, and the checkered, blue hospital gown with the putrid stain, that had made me gag only hours before, would be thrown into a mountain of soiled linen in a giant hospital laundry to be disinfected, to be purified. I wondered if the hand of the angel of death would wipe the blemishes and lesions from the dead man's skin before his corpse was rolled into the crematorium oven.

I was standing by one of my windows, looking across the wide Soho street toward the multistoried, sandblasted facades of the Beaux Arts buildings, industrial contemporaries of the domestic architecture of the unlucky Park Slope house.

It was Friday evening, only weeks before Christmas. In the now sought after expensive living spaces in their glow of lights, I could glimpse through windows directly facing mine, the comings and goings of a fashionably dressed group of people at a festive gathering, in a luxuriously put together interior. Clinking glasses. Kissing cheeks. Or the air near them. During holiday time there would be many parties such as this. Filled with chatter and laughter, and the making of plans, disagreements, lover's quarrels ….,

I had forgotten the telephone receiver in my hand. Jerry was still on the line:

"He was a very special man," he was saying. "I am sorry for your loss...."

I could have done without "sorry for your loss."

I could have done without "they were helping him pass."

I could have done without Jerry's voice in my ear.

I should have been there, I thought.

I hung up.

ONCE UPON A TIME...AND LATER

PIPER CUB

1.

Thanksgiving afternoon Billy climbed into the cockpit of his yellow Piper Cub at Rutland airport and fifteen minutes later landed the plane on a plowed, empty farmer's field in Castleton, directly behind his former English professor's house surprising him, his wife, their two teenaged sons and several dinner guests just as they were finishing a traditional, overstuffed turkey meal.

Billy had been Henry's favorite student at the college. His welcoming wife Regina, round and comfy, enjoyed the company of most of her husband's students. But none more than that of charming Billy. His unexpected arrival by air infused a fresh spark into the onset of a soporific mood around the Thanksgiving holiday table.

After sampling slices of Regina's pumpkin and apple pies, and amusing the now somewhat revived guests, Billy zipped up his father's WW2 bomber jacket, wrapped his white aviator scarf around his neck, walked out of the house and climbed back into his little yellow biplane. He turned on the motor and waved goodbye to Regina and Henry, their two teenaged sons and guests who watched from the back porch as the golden boy revved up his plane to make it lift from the misty grey field toward the sky. No leaves on the trees. November.

When the Piper Cub went into a funny spin, all those on the ground thought that Billy was signing off with a small air show. Within seconds the plane nosedived onto the barren, autumn brown earth behind Henry's and Regina's house.

The professor's two teenaged boys pulled Billy out of the crumbled wreckage just as it was ready to burst into flames. In no time the local volunteer fire crew and ambulance were on the scene. The medics gathered the bloodied body of the unconscious flyer onto a stretcher they placed in the emergency vehicle and sped away.

The next day and for several weeks after the Thanksgiving Day accident, the front pages of Vermont newspapers were full of reports of the crash and the condition of the local aviator. The impact of the crash had been swift and violent. There were pictures of the crushed Piper Cub loaded onto the back of a flatbed truck. The yellow biplane looked like a piece of crumpled origami not folded quite right. Next to the instrument panel, Billy's face had left a clear impression on the dashboard. The hospital bulletins posted slim expectations for his survival.

Henry, a poet and classics professor, had been my husband's best friend since their high school days. He introduced his student to us at the lake house we had rented for the summer several years before the accident.

Billy was a beauty. Tall, strong, sinewy, with smooth silky skin. An abundant fringe of blond hair, soft as a baby's, teased his forehead above blue, blue eyes. There was always something vulnerable in his posture and conversation. He displayed no arrogance or any hint of being aware of his great, good looks. He had been an athlete in high school. In season he hunted deer with his father. Since he had become a college student, Billy's interests gravitated toward books. He read history and classical and contemporary literature. When we met he kept reading and rereading "Lolita" and novels by Jerzy Koszinsky.

To the country boy we were news, fast and fascinating city art people. He was seduced by all four of us. My ten year old boy liked Billy and looked up to him. My thirteen year old daughter and her giggling girl friends visiting from New York City, loved to tease him. Delighting him at the thought of having come face to face with real Nabokovian nymphets. I hoped I didn't qualify as the "Haze woman."

With sun bronzed skin, in a bikini with a rope of hippie beads dangling from my neck, I played the freewheeling summer hostess. With the help of my Julia Child cook books I was prepared to entertain. At the makeshift stove I cooked and baked and served up meals to friends new and old who never said "no" to the summer fun always available at our rented lake house. We drank cool gin drinks and consumed bottles of wine and cases of beer and smoked joints and worshipped the Beatles newly released "Sergeant Pepper"…and swayed and rocked to Dylan and the "Dead" and jumped in the lake. Some evenings we piled into cars and went dancing at a local dive, where everyone knew the guys in the band.

"Billy is sweet on you," Regina whispered to me one day. "It's obvious. You must sense it yourself."

I laughed. "Sweet on me!" I liked the quaint, American country expression. I was the cool, older, married city woman. He was the vision of innocent country youth. "Sweet on me" was nice. But dangerous too. Billy, "attainable" during this summer interlude could lead to trouble.

The sun shimmering on the lake and the light of the summer moon and the frequent presence of Billy revived and compensated for memories of a much younger me. The me before I had become a wife and mother. The me, who in Stockholm, Sweden, had been a fifteen year old high school girl who once had a painful wild crush on an unattainable, beautiful blond student who ran the other way each time he thought I was approaching him in the schoolyard.

Time moves at a different pace when it marches to a predetermined ending marked on the calendar. In fields the tiger lilies were closing up their season. The arrival of fresh corn and zucchini began to fill the farmers' stands by the roadside. By the lake it was easy to be aware of the sun sinking just a little earlier each evening. These were daily reminders of the shrinking times still left of summer.

"We got here only yesterday," I said to my husband. "Where did it all go?"

"I've had enough," he said, not really surprising me. He was busy wrapping up the pictures for the book he had found time to work on at the makeshift, shaky table. Sweeping us and the summer out of the house by the lake, he mumbled, "I am more than ready to be back home at my own desk."

All the regulars were invited to a goodbye dinner. There had to be a last farewell staged to honor the magical summer before we emptied the house and left it to falling leaves and the hunting season and then snow. September winds were rattling the window panes, penetrating indoors and threatening to blow out candles I had set up on a board that served as an improvised dinner table. I had prepared beouf bourgignon and au gratin potatoes. A green salad and cheeses followed. Plenty of white and red wine had been passed around. For desert I had made a tarte au pommes and madelaines, the little "memory" cakes my son called "mama's Proust cookies."

Henry and Regina brought their two boys. So little then. And such terrors, years before they had grown into the strapping jocks who pulled Billy out of the burning Piper Cub. At our good-byes we all shed drunken tears and promises to stay in touch forever.

After everyone stumbled into cars and left, after my husband and the children went to sleep, after I left the dishes in the sink for the next morning, Billy lingered. He stacked logs in the fireplace and lit a fire.

We smoked joints and got giggly and hungry and picked on leftovers. The rock music we played quietly on a local station, expanded from a center of sound into wave upon wave until I thought I was floating inside of it. I saw dancers and roses cavorting in the flames.

"Look, Billy," I whispered, once again delighting in the taste of his name on my lips. "Look. This is better than a lightshow!" I don't know if he saw any pictures in the flames. He didn't say.

When the fire began to die down and he didn't revive it with a fresh log, I wanted to cry: Make it burn longer, Billy Goat. Or throw me in the back of your pick-up truck, and carry me far, far away from sleeping husband and children, deep into the Vermont woods and lay me down on a bed of moss and don't let anyone find us.

I had to settle for a farewell to the romance that never was.

It was then. It was over. It was all.

Back in Brooklyn, we did stay in touch with our country boy Billy. He had been the first to write. Charming and witty letters. On the surface, they were addressed to all four of us. But, here and there, I found a phrase that could only have been meant for me. Like reminiscing about the time the two of us had snuck away to swim all the way to the other side of the lake without telling anyone. In spite of the rule that no one playing or staying with us at the lake house was allowed to do such a thing without an escort following in a row boat for protection. I wanted to write back as soon as I had read his letter, but I forced myself to let a little time pass before I wrote a carefully crafted, chatty response.

And then, Billy began to travel. He had often talked about wanting to extend his life to worlds away from Vermont lakes and woods. When local friends, who had joined the Peace Corps, ended up doing good works in Kabul, invited him to stay with them, he jumped at the chance to explore Afghanistan. When he passed through New York and walked into our newly acquired Victorian house it took me a moment to displace him from the plein-air of the summer landscape and put him into the hermetic indoors of our city dwelling. New setting or not, there he was in the flesh. My heart skipped a beat. I took cover behind food preparation and brittle chatter.

Months later, on his return from the Middle East, Billy strolled in wearing an Afghan hat and flowing robes, looking like Peter O'Toole in "Lawrence of Arabia." He had made friends with tribal Afghans and recovered from dysentery. He had watched the sun rise over Khyber Pass. He brought camel bags and small native rugs as presents. Things he was planning to import. The time was right for selling such artifacts.

In Vermont Billy had his own way of acquiring and distributing goods. He had once brought Henry an almost new lawn mower. His professor would have liked to have kept the questionably-acquired present, but he couldn't see himself putt-putting around, being visible on the plot of grass surrounding his house, perhaps having the rightful owner drive by one day and recognize the machine. Billy was thanked for his thoughtfulness. The lawn mower was loaded back onto his old pick-up truck, covered with a blanket and returned, under the cover of darkness, to the barn from which it had been lifted.

Before the end of that summer, Billy had presented me with a full length mirror in an ornate, gaudy, slightly cracked, antique gilt frame.

"I found it in an abandoned mansion," he told us.

My husband did not think we should accept it.

I had no such problem. There was no way that I would refuse the offering.

As far as I was concerned, Billy's local robberies were innocent, generous pranks, with no resemblance to crime.

Billy's international travels did not end with Afghanistan. Soon his travels extended to jetting on the Concorde to London and on to Nigeria. Once, before leaving after a short stay with us, he left a Baretta in a holster on our dining room table.

"Aren't you forgetting something?" my husband said handing the pistol to the wandering boy before driving him to the airport.

I never found out how Billy had advanced from lawn mower and mirror pilfering in an unlocked Vermont barn or crumbling, abandoned mansion, to the wheeling and dealing of an international soldier of fortune. I never learned what else, besides Afghan rugs and camel bags, Billy was importing.

"Better we don't know," my husband said. "In case whatever he is doing leads to some future questioning involving us."

I didn't disagree. My husband wasn't wrong. But, I wanted to tell him, that he was a prig!

When the traveler passed through again dressed in tribal garb or a new suit from Saville Row, I couldn't avoid that flare-up of my old summer crush. Remembering those moments when I heard the unmistakable sound of the rattle of his pick-up truck turning from the road onto the parking spot behind the lake house. Now, Billy's boyish country sheen, was enhanced by the new ease with which he dashed back and forth to Europe and Africa.

During one of his New York stopovers, right after my husband and I had settled into our big 19th Century house, sufficiently distanced from him at work at his desk in our top floor studio, Billy pulled me behind the door of the small dark pantry by the side of the kitchen, and swept me into his arms. Embraced in the fresh, clean smell of his body, his mouth open, his wet tongue pushing, melting into my mouth, I could have said that he was overwhelming me. That would not have been true. The moment did not feel surprising. Since I had first met Billy, I had imagined and staged and tasted such moments in my mind and body so often, that I felt this was not the first time, that it had already happened many times before.

We stayed like that, kissing and groping like a couple of teens, hiding from an oblivious parent in another part of the house. His arms around me, the sweetness of his breath, the taste of his mouth were summer treasures. Stored and left behind, Billy was retrieving imagined moments for us from where they had been tucked away at the end of the summer, untouched, unspoiled, in the hollow of a tree, or under a stone by the dock, at the end of the summer by the lake. To me our little tryst had nothing to do with cheating any more than Billy's helping himself to a lawn mower or an old mirror had to do with crime.

And then, Billy did surprise me, "On my next trip," he whispered,. "I'll be on my way back from Geneva." I held my breath. "Why don't you meet me in Paris?"

I saw us as if in a slow panning shot in a film romance emerging from the greenery in Vermont or from a dark corner behind the pantry door in a Brooklyn house, into an elegant bedroom in a small Paris hotel with Toile de Jouy wallpaper, with soft curtains wafting in the windows, and in the distance, a view of the Dome of Les Invalides or the Eiffel Tower.... Why not, I thought? There would be nothing suspect in my suggesting to my husband that I take a quick trip to Paris by myself. I, the Francophile, had done that before. It posed no threat to his and my unshakable, solid long marriage.

We heard my husband's footsteps on the stairs and pulled apart. I hurried to the kitchen to get busy with the coffee maker.

A few days after the secret smooching, I called Billy in Vermont. I had come up with a date that would coincide with his leaving Geneva. As soon as I heard his voice at the end of the line, I regretted making the call.

His stay in Geneva was being prolonged, he said. He was not sure that he could get away to Paris after all.

He needed to hurry back to Vermont. I should have known that our giddy, sweet, unplanned moment behind the pantry door could not hold up in a negotiation for a French tryst. The adventurer, may have been "sweet on me," once. Maybe still was. But, when faced with really betraying the married man, who was his friend, who took time away from his work to drive him to the airport after his visits, country gentleman Billy backed away. Shamelessly ready to jump into an invitation to adventure and romance, I had laid myself bare and invited rejection.

Time passed. Billy's stopovers in Brooklyn became less and less frequent until they ceased altogether. There was nothing but silence. Henry and Regina had also not heard much from him.

One day an important looking envelope arrived in the mail. On textured off white, grainy, linen paper. With all the proper inserts for RSVP printed in gilt cursive lettering: "Mr. and Mrs. so-and-so request the pleasure of your company at the nuptials of their daughter, Britney…. To William…. etc.etc.etc…."

My husband was disappointed that magical Billy was entering into "nuptials" with a local girl named Britney.

"I was sure," he surprised me by saying, "That if he ever got married, it would be to some interesting European woman."

I had to veil my sadness with propriety. I went to Tiffany's and bought two exquisite, stemmed Waterford glasses. We sent the wedding present and our best wishes along with our regrets.

It was mid September. Already red and gold leaves were waving in the breeze and falling on the Vermont landscape. The wedding ceremony was an outdoor event on the grounds of a well known mansion with some historic significance. There were tents and torches and urns filled with masses of autumn flowers and white ribbons and rosettes tied around the white, wooden folding chairs. More than a hundred guests had been invited. After the two B's had said their vows, two small planes flew overhead and made loop-de-loops in honor of Billy, who after taking flying lessons, had just passed his pilot's license. His instructors and flying buddies were honoring and welcoming the new aviator to the air.

Then a storm of hurricane proportions descended, tearing covers off the tents, overturning flower urns and chairs and service tables, sending wedding guests, local and international, for cover inside the mansion.

All this we heard later from Regina and Henry, who had gone to the wedding.

"Several of Billy's former girl friends came," Regina laughed. "They stumbled around, very drunk and stoned. They were not having a good time."

I was glad that my husband and I had skipped Billy's wedding to Britney.

The young marrieds, we heard, went to Switzerland to ski that winter. They met an American plastic surgeon who attached himself to this attractive couple. Especially to the husband. Sometime later, I saw a picture of the surgeon posing with Billy and Britney in matching tuxedos at a New Year's Eve gala at the fancy Alpine hotel where they were all staying. Britney decided to have the surgeon do her nose job when they returned to the States.

In Vermont, way up on a mountain, architects and builders had begun work on the remodeling of the house Billy had bought for himself and his bride. There were to be windows all around with faraway mountain views. There was to be a hot tub on the deck. In the garage there was a Porsche, a Mercedes convertible, a fancy jeep. In a hangar at the Rutland airport, Billy kept a small jet plane and a Piper Cub. In Vermont, at the time of his crash, he was a visible gentleman of means.

Billy was in a coma. Surgeons had removed his right eye. The damaged optical nerves threatened the survival of the left eye. Just above the anklebone, his left foot had snapped to a ninety degree angle. It was reset with screws and a steel plate. The plastic surgeon from the skiing trip in Switzerland flew in from LA to operate and rearrange Billy's crushed face.

"If he recovers," one surgeon told Britney, "he will be crippled and legally blind for the rest of his life."

Billy surprised them all. After three weeks he woke from his coma, sat up in bed and began to joke with nurses and doctors and medical personnel, questioning the fuss all around him. Nothing had happened to his mouth. No teeth had been broken. After a stint at an institute for the blind and another at a rehab center with intense physical therapy, he was discharged and began his recovery. Before long he went home to his wife on crutches.

I was living alone now. In my busy, unexpected bachelor life in Manhattan, I had found consolations. This was the wild and wicked 80ties. After so many years with one man, a new male person in my bed, now and then, was an amusing and welcome surprise. Since my split from my husband and domesticity in Brooklyn, there had been several. Picked up in bars. Young. Callow. Inane. Delicious. "Das schönste am Welt ist Liebe, und am Morgen denkt man da nichts," goes the bitter song from the Brecht/Weill "Mahogany." But I did think about them after they closed the door behind them in the morning. And I hoped maybe this one or that one would call and come through the door again.

Thoughts of my non-romance with Billy had become sediments buried beneath more recent hurts and upheavals. I had indulged in that fantasy within the shelter of what I had believed, had been the solid and unshakable, good marriage. Which, in the end, my husband and I had, each of us in our own way, whittled away with dull knives.

One dark, late afternoon in October there was a phone call from Billy.

"I am at La Guardia," he said. "I'll be catching the shuttle to Boston tomorrow afternoon. Can I come to…….." I didn't let him finish the sentence.

"Oh, please, you must ..." I gave him directions to my place. "Come! I can't wait to see you."

I ran to Dean & DeLuca. I bought pate and cheeses, a baguette and giant California strawberries with their stems still on. At the wine shop I bought a bottle of Dom Perignon and a bottle of red wine.

Setting out the food, the plates, glasses and linen napkins on the large glass coffee table in my glossy Soho apartment, a compressed, terrifying, roped-in sensation, that could only be compared to stage fright, seized me.

More than three years had passed since that stormy wedding I had skipped. I hadn't had any contact with him since before the crash. I had to force myself to think of this visit as a meeting of two old friends. Two friends whose lives had been turned upside down.

"He is not the man he used to be," Regina had told me not long ago. I had not seen any recent photos of him. I was scared of my reaction to the apparition that would soon be arriving on my doorstep.

Stop this nonsense, I tried to calm myself. A crippled, half blind, married man I couldn't even call an "old flame" is dropping in on his way home to his wife in Vermont. Stop being silly. Take a bath. Serve him food and drink. Play the hostess.

I followed my advice. Took a shower. Washed my hair. Dressed in a short skirt and a silk shirt. Good black stockings. Elegant flats. My hands shook when I was putting on make-up. When the buzzer rang. I took a quick look in the ornate gilt framed mirror, the Billy gift, stolen and carried away from a Vermont barn that magic summer by the lake.

"I'll be right down," I thrilled into the intercom. Ignoring the elevator, I ran down the three flights of stairs.

On crutches, in flowing white robes, a pirate's black patch covering his empty right eye socket, stood Lawrence of Arabia once again. The doorman had helped him out of the cab into the vestibule.

I took his bag. I helped him into the elevator. There was a cumbersome leather brace on his injured left leg. He lumbered down the hall between two crutches, making a strange circular motion with the braced leg.

We hugged. Old friends. Long time no see. Changes. The crippled adventurer had managed a trip from Vermont to St Vincent and to Florida and was making a stop in Soho, New York City, to see me. He peered at me with his one eye.

"You look beautiful," he said. I knew I had been renewed in my recent life. To his limited vision the unmarried me, in fresh, new surroundings, no doubt did not look bad.

We sat on my new Italian leather couch. We sampled pate and cheeses set out on my new glass coffee table. We dipped our strawberries in the champagne. We tried to be normal old friends, chatting about the crazy twists and turns in our lives that had brought us to this moment.

There were several phone calls from Britney that evening. Of course, she was worried. Her husband traveling alone in his condition. Getting in and out of airplanes and taxis. But she couldn't possibly suspect that her crippled husband would share anything but food and conversation with his old friend.

I had met Britney only once, when I spent a weekend with Regina and Henry in Vermont not long after my husband and I had separated. The professor and his wife had invited the young marrieds over for drinks. I had no idea during my first meeting with Billy's bride, the local girl who had landed a catch, whether she was presenting a face before or after her nose job. The newlyweds were both wearing slim jeans and western shirts. On Billy the outfit made a fashion statement. On Britney the exact same garments looked plain and ordinary. As if it she had gone shopping at the local WalMart. Sitting side by side on the couch in Regina's and Henry's book filled, cluttered living room, I did not think I was in the presence of a married couple, but rather a brother and his much, much plainer, unremarkable younger sister.

On my couch in Soho Billy took off his rolled Afghan cap. Part of his soft blond hair above his forehead had been shaved for the operations. A graphic scar, a thin, fading red line, extended from ear to ear. I cradled his head and began to cry. He kissed me the way he had kissed me behind the pantry door in the house in Park Slope.

"Everything of importance still works," he quipped.

The brace on his leg had to be carefully unstrapped before we lay down on my bed together for the first time. There followed a night of cautious positioning and delicate clinging and polite moaning. His ardor was exaggerated. Mine over compensating. I was a refugee from a shriveled marriage. Billy was married and crushed. Both of us labored bravely at this long delayed seduction. In the morning I helped him into the shower. I helped him shave. We were cheerful and felt rakish about having spent such a forbidden "erotic" night together, at last. I called for a limousine and rode with him to the airport with the leftover red wine and snacks in a picnic basket between us.

"Shall we stay in touch?" I asked. The hoped for, reassuring response, did not come. I instantly regretted what I had said. "Or is that not in the script?"

"I am afraid it can't be in the script," the now somewhat tarnished gentleman Billy answered.

At La Guardia, I helped him fill out the boarding pass for the Boston shuttle, and escorted him to the gate. In my bedroom I took a moment before I began to straighten and smooth the crumpled sheets. I didn't change them. Married Billy was up in the air returning to Vermont to his married life with Britney. It was not exactly fitting to compare myself to the bride whose second biggest disappointment in life had been Niagara Falls.

After that visit I heard not a word from Billy. I depended on reports from Regina and Henry. He had begun to drink heavily. With his limited vision and drunk, he would jump into one of his cars and drive away in the snow. He would leave his new glass eyeball in a place where Britney could easily spot it. Once he drove one of his cars into a tree and got stuck in a snowdrift. His wife came with friends and chains in a truck to get him and pull the car out. They kept the incident hushed to avoid police and insurance agents.

    Several months after our pathetic night together, the law did catch up with charming Billy. He had strutted in a small community in a small state. After the reports of his plane crash and miraculous recovery buzzed in the local newspapers, he had become notorious. The IRS came to the door to demand answers to how all this visible money had been earned. And, why no taxes had been paid on any of it.

    Billy's physical condition served him well at the Grand Jury hearings. He narrowly avoided incarceration in one of those elegant gentleman prisons. The fine house with the hot tub and the view and the land that stretched through one hundred acres of Vermont fields and woods were confiscated.

    He did manage to squirrel away some gemstones and a collection of fine Japanese prints. And some money in a London bank account. He sold his Porsche to a guy in the area with the idea that he might buy it back some day. He was allowed to keep the Mercedes. Sweet, unremarkable Britney ran away with the man who had been Billy's best man at their wedding.

    I had just returned from the awful visit to the hospital when he rang my doorbell and reappeared in my life again. More than a year had passed since Billy and I had spent that night of clumsy, groping coupling in my bed. That evening we sat across the table from each other in a Japanese restaurant in Soho. He was savoring sashimi. I barely tasted my favorite, delicately seasoned portions of maki rolls and side dish of tempura. We were sipping warmed sake out of exquisite little earthenware cups.

Billy was healed as far as he would heal. His walking was normal. He could run and he could ski again, he said. The empty socket of his dead eye was filled with a beautiful, porcelain prosthesis, a perfect match to his real blue eye. In it the vision had been restored almost completely. He was wearing glasses. His elegant mouth and the curve of his strong chin were unchanged.

Oh, but he was handsome! In a new way. In his face, sadder, wiser, not perfect, I searched for the long gone faun who had walked into my life one carefree summer by a Vermont lake.

In the light of a small paper lantern, Billy leaned close to me across the table and whispered, "I love you." Lifting his cup of sake, he added, "I have always loved you."

A gulp from my sake mingled in my mouth with the taste of the sweet country expression from a long time ago. "And I never stopped being sweet on you," I said softly.

It was simple. It was enough. It was now.

PARIS INTERLUDE

Waiting

1.

The balmy spring day in May I was spending alone in Paris was not the one I had planned or wished for.

Nevertheless, throughout the morning, I did an obedient, systematic stroll turning corners, nodding silent greetings to familiar sights in areas of the Left Bank. I stopped in the still empty Luxembourg garden remembering the time, not so long ago, when surly old ladies dressed in black collected payment before a person was permitted to sit down in one of those metal chairs.

I waited for the museum to open so I could wander for a while among the small dense, dark mysteries of Redon paintings and graphics currently on exhibition.

That done, I sauntered toward Boulevard Saint Germain. In a favorite boutique on Rue Saint Peres I tried on a pair of white linen pants and a midnight blue silk shirt. I couldn't resist buying both.

On Quai Voltaire, in the old art store where I always stopped to buy a few fine watercolor brushes ever since I discovered it on my very first trip to Paris, I came across a surprising little wooden box with a sliding cover that housed a neatly packed set of miniature alphabet blocks.

I crossed the river on Pont Saint Philippe to the short street that bears the same name as the bridge, and was reassured that the store where I liked to buy handmade paper was still there. And it was open.

"Vous parlez bien Francais, Madame," the salesclerk said, while he helped me pull out sheets of paper. The French always compliment one, as if they can't quite accept that now and then an American is able to wrap a tongue around their language. By way of prolonging for myself a little chatter in French, I told the young man that I had attended classes at the Sorbonne. That I read books in French. That I often took quick trips to Paris. That I lived in New York.

"Vous avez de la chance, madame," he sighed. Adding that he longed to take a trip to New York City. Maybe before too long.

While I watched him carefully roll up my papers and slide them into a tube, I was projecting myself into the moment at home when the papers were going to be unrolled onto my drawing desk and I would begin to mess the unspoiled, slightly crinkly surfaces with brushstrokes of paint.

My determination to fill my day with activities, not much different from those that occupied my days in Paris during other visits short or long, was keeping brooding at bay.

In late afternoon, I stopped at a bistro on a side street off the Avenue de L'Opéra to eat a steak frites and drink a glass of red wine. Fortified, I continued my walk in the direction of Palais Royal.

At the *Comédie Française* I bought a ticket in the *parterre* for that evening's performance of *"École des Femmes."*

The *Comédie* actors are always wonderful to listen to, but this performance of the Moliere play in a modern dress interpretation by a new young director from the Netherlands turned out to be an aggressively jarring mishmash, forced and irritating.

On the way back to my hotel, while passing the Louvre I paused to contemplate the glass pyramid. So playful and scintillating in the moonlight. So settled and secure in the center between the severe stony walls of the ancient edifice. What a brouhaha there had been in Paris when the contemporary intrusion had been originally conceived and erected. Hitler did not level Paris. I.M. Pei did not insult it.

At last permitting myself to anticipate the message that would surely be waiting for me at reception, as I turned the corner to Rue Cassette I passed, leaning against the wrought iron gate of an elegant 17th century hotel particulier, a Harley Davidson motorcycle. The light from the carefully recreated gaslight glow of a contemporary Parisian electric streetlamp reflected in the paint and chrome of the shiny powerful machine. The handlebars extended in a wide, elegant port-de-bras, seemingly welcoming the rider into an embrace, promising adventure. And danger.

I remembered that I never said "no" to the motor-cycle rides in New York City when the Polish boy from Detroit appeared, often unannounced, at my door.

"My Hog is waiting, fancy lady," he would say. "Let's ride!"

Those night rides ceased when the rider had to sell his motorcycle to pay off drug debts and get out of town to escape from drug dealers and the police. That romance, never over-burdened with expectations, came to its predictable end.

In the vestibule of Hotel de L'Abbaye on the peach-colored wall hangs a large, late Post Impressionist painting of a courtesan in deshabille reclining on a bed among dissheveled sheets. A black suited gentleman with a shiny top hat already poised on his head is preparing to make an exit. In his hand he holds a wad of bills ready to be tossed on the frilly night table.

At reception the night porter handed me my room key. *"Bonne nuit, madame,"* he smiled. *"Dormez bien."*

There was no mention of a message.

The man could not know that this 'dame,' exhausted from a full day of Parisian wanderings and doings, was heading for the little cage elevator that would ascend with her to the top floor, where she would open the door to the pink Toile de Jouy papered room, and find a chocolate on the pillow and climb alone under the satiny cover and fine sheets, only to toss and turn and try to make excuses for Monsieur who wasn't there.

And where she would most likely not spend a "good night" or "sleep well."

After only one day my long wished for first romantic Paris trip with Billy had been interrupted by an unanticipated phone call.

It came from his Greek friend, a member of a shipping family, who happened to be in London. A meeting with a maritime engineer from a shipyard company in Scotland had been arranged. Billy was attempting to rekindle business relationships with past international contacts. The Greek friend knew he was going to be in Paris. Wouldn't this be a fine time to have a meeting in London to pitch the joint venture they had been discussing? To propose the production of leisure submarines for underwater tourism?

"You say how easy it is for you to have a great time by yourself in Paris," Billy, excited, packing an overnight bag, was saying to me. "You are at home here."

To prove that I was "at home" in Paris by myself had not been the purpose of this trip.

Getting into the taxi for the airport early the next morning, "I'll probably stay with a friend," he said.

He had mentioned a girlfriend from his jet-setting days who had an apartment in London.

"I'll call," was the last thing he said before shutting the taxi door.

Not a glance back.

Not a word from him since he left.

I hesitated by the elevator. I would leave my packages with the porter, return my key, walk away from the hotel and duck into some bar in the area. I would order a strong drink and send signals as obvious and inviting as Christmas decorations to make myself available to n'importe quel mec. If I were lucky, I might stumble upon a French version of my Polish motorcycle swain from Detroit.

Or, what if I went back to the corner of Rue Cassette to stand under the streetlight where the Harley was parked? What if the owner sensed my presence and emerged into his courtyard as handsome and as sleek as his shiny machine?

"Venez, chere madame," he would point to the Harley, inviting me to settle my derriere on his chrome horse.

Off we would ride, speeding on the empty wide boulevards and narrow streets of nighttime Paris.

The ride I took was the one in the cage elevator to the top floor. I opened the door to my room. It was late. Even in Paris, everyone who needed to, or was lucky enough, or was obligated to, must have paired up for the night. I no longer expected the phone to ring. It was too late for phone calls. For wild times. For anything. Tossing and turning in bed in a room in the elegant small Left Bank hotel in Paris was a reminder of similar dark nights of the soul in the marital king-sized bed in the large master bedroom in the elegant house in Park Slope, Brooklyn.

In the pink room with frolicking shepherds and shepherdesses I smoked many Gauloises. Welcoming their sharp, honest attack on my throat.

Bonne nuit, Madame, dormez bien, was not going to be.

I was once again the woman who waits.

I hear police car sirens approaching, coming closer. Billy stands in the middle of the room. His head reaches the ceiling. Both of his eyes are empty sockets.

His lips are forming into a funnel. Now he is blowing into a conch. A hollow, thin, mournful sound is coming out of him. I turn my head to the wall. I don't want to look at him. I don't want to listen to him. Then I hear a loud rush of cascading water. I am standing by the bathroom door watching my dead husband in blue striped pajamas kneel on the tiled floor. His head is hanging over the rim of the bathtub. Water is pouring out of his eyes.

    I was wakened by the soprano bell chime of the phone on the bed side table.
    "Good morning, little mouse," Billy's voice caressed my ear. "I just landed."
    Trying not to burst into tears, I don't know what I babbled at him. I was wide awake.
    "The deal looks very promising," he went on." I can't wait to tell you! ...And, I do have a surprise for us."
    I threw myself into the shower. Washed my hair and rinsed away blackish thoughts and suspicions. I dressed in my new soft white linen pants and midnight blue silk shirt.
    I opened the wooden box I had bought and tossed out the little alphabet blocks on the front of the dresser. I had just enough time to arrange:
    'welcomebackbillygoatlovemouse'
    The door opened.
    There he was.

After a week of perfect days in Paris, walking, eating, sipping wine, falling into bed to make love, giggling, we flew to Athens.

Docked at a marina in Piraeus, Billy's Greek friends had made available to us their fully equipped small yacht and its crew. For the next two weeks we sailed and visited islands of the Aegean.

I stopped being the woman who waits.

EPILOGUE

A CHRISTMAS UP NORTH

𝓕or several years now, Billy's aunt has asked us to come and spend Christmas with her.

"You know she'll be alone, as always," I said. "We talk about it every year. Shouldn't we finally do it?"

By mid November my dread of the obligations to festivities of the season begins. Plans have to be made so as not to be left out. I wish to fit in with all the others who might easily pirouette through the year end of feasts, of songs and of lights that blink in the night. Christmas has layers of memories sweet and sad, joyous and horrific. I want to be one of the people who pile into cars and airplanes, just because they have been invited somewhere or bought themselves a place to go to. How often isn't it a chore? How often aren't prescriptions of good will and good times a trap. I have wrestled my life away from many such conventions. But Christmas claims me. At Christmas I want a vacation from my self-inflicted freedoms.

I am not in mourning for the gone domestic scene with husband and children, the important carefully wrapped presents hidden in secret nooks and crannies until they were brought out and arranged under the tree on Christmas Eve. And the "oohs" and "aahs" resounding on Christmas morning when the family unwrapping ritual began. No, I don't long for that.

I don't long for the days before Christmas Day when I went into battle preparing and baking pates and pickled shrimp. Planning the ham or pork roast. Italian pasta dishes and Christmas sweets. And, torrents of liquor calculated for around forty guests. With all that I had sugared the nagging doubts, that my life ought not to be the one I lived in that big house, on the wide tree lined street. I don't want those old times back. I don't. But the memories of those days, and older barren, evil ones from even longer past, do haunt me.

These days I plan a quieter December 25th, a very miniature version of my old Christmas hoopla. Billy and I invite two or three friends who have bowed out of obligatory family invitations, or those who may have had none at all.

Our Christmas holiday celebration has fallen into a quiet event without the taint of hysteria of my old hoopla. Yes, we do have a small nicely decorated tree. Yes, there are presents. Christmas Eve, Billy waits by the fire for my return from Midnight Mass at a neighborhood church with Japanese snacks and sake.

Christmas Day I cook; we invite two or three friends who have bowed out of obligatory family invitations, or who may have had none at all.

"This year I would like to cook Christmas dinner at your aunt's," I say. "Don't you think that will be very nice?"

"Well, think about it." Billy attempts to shield me from my machinations in the direction of seasonal goodwill. "How long do you think you'll be able to stand Anna's fussing and fluttering?"

I dismissed Billy's concern. "Haven't you noticed that when we are together, Anna and I always find things to talk about."

Yes, that was true. We did. So much so, that I have often felt like the second old lady in the room. Two old ladies chattering about things that are of no interest to him. Certainly, without the vestige of my Christmas obsession, Billy would gladly ignore the whole frenzied season altogether.

Billy made the call to his aunt. "She wants you to order a goose," he was saying.

I was listening on the extension.

"A goose!, Oh, goodness,..yes!" Billy's Aunt Anna, as if on cue, was already being Anna, fluttering at the other end of the line.

"She had never had goose for Christmas. "This will be, yes… Willy,..a new experience for me….Yes!"

Billy assured her that I would do all the cooking. That we would be paying for all the food.

It was decided. We were going to Hanover, New Hampshire for Christmas.

Out of my Swedish cookbook I copied the roasting directions for goose as well as for the red cabbage and glazed potatoes. Taking my little scenario on tour was the perfect antidote to potential Christmas sadness. I was going to find fresh salvation by preparing holiday food in Billy's aunt's kitchen.

The decision was settling. When asked by friends or neighbors in New York City, I found relief in saying, quietly, or viva voce: "We are going away. North. To snow. To New England. And you? Oh, how nice. Blah. Blah. Merry Christmas. Happy New Year."

The 45 minute flight from Kennedy on Jet Blue deposited us at Burlington, Vermont, airport. As soon as we were on the ground Billy called his aunt.
"She has picked up the goose," he said.
We stepped out of the terminal heading for the parking lot. Our breath curled out of our lungs, meeting the pristine cold, cold air. Our rented car waited in the designated Avis spot. We settled into the front seats. The two of us rolling down the road again through the unsunny landscape of winter in New England. Inside the car we were warm and cozy. I turned on the radio. It was Christmas Eve afternoon. Christmas choir music transformed the rented vehicle into a concert hall on wheels. I loved looking at Billy's strong, beautiful hands on the steering wheel. Our Soho life, enhanced with impulsive trips to Paris or London or Stockholm, as well as summer stays in Vermont, had settled into our own reasonable calm without ever losing the glow of romance. We were happy.
At the door to her ground floor condo, properly located near the campus of Dartmouth in Hanover, Aunt Anna, very thin and trim, bunny slippers on her feet, enveloped in a big sweater, embraced us both with the anticipated flurry of: "This is great, oh.,. yes, ..this is nice.. You see,. yes.. I am so glad… " She fussed and

chirped: "Welcome,. Yes...Yes, this is really Christmas... Yes."

We arranged our sleeping bags in the small, rarely used guest room and unpacked some extra clothes and the presents we had brought.

"Your package from California arrived," Anna said.

I had asked my son and daughter-in-law to mail their presents for Billy and me to New Hampshire. Quite a few boxes in shiny wrappings and ribbons were arranged under the leafy plant, decorated with blinking white lights. It was not a half-bad compromise, standing in for a Christmas tree. Anna had opened the big FedEx box and freed the presents from bubble wraps and clinging Styrofoam peanuts. We added our few gifts to the others beneath the ersatz tree. Big, strangely lugubrious looking thick candles, quite a few of them, were arranged on tables and shelves.

"Now I'll get rid of all this junk," Billy said, moving resolutely toward the mailing cartons that were piled up by the entrance door to the apartment. He crushed the boxes and packing materials before carrying armfuls of the stuff out to the garbage dumpsters in the enclosed shed by the side of the parking lot available to the condo residents. The semicircular condominium of two story units is neat and proper and safe and quiet as death.

After the warm embraces and Anna's giddy delight at having her darling Willy and his lady friend, to spend holiday time with, I gave Billy a quick glance "See, I was right!"

I went to survey the kitchen. It was obvious that I would have to make do with the electric stove, thin pots and dull lightweight knives that were not exactly chef cuisiniere equipment. Along with the goose, Billy had asked Anna to pick up potatoes, the head of red cabbage, onions and apples the day before. It could wait but, I wanted to do some prepping ahead of the Christmas Day cooking. I chopped and peeled and tossed and seasoned and put the Swedish red cabbage mixture on a low setting in the oven to simmer. Anna fluttered and prattled and was content to do the cleaning up of scraps on the counter and from the floor.

The darkening late afternoon was filling with the holiday smells remembered from other times. In my mind I was still preparing quantities of food suitable for more than three people. In cooking, the large head of cabbage shrank considerably. I finished by letting it simmer on the electric burner on top of the stove. Before refrigerating the concoction, Anna and I dipped into it and decided that the Swedish sweet and sour traditional dish had turned out well. Later we reheated some of the cabbage and served it with baked potatoes and the quickly grilled small steaks of an indeterminate cut, Anna had supplied for Christmas Eve dinner.

Even though I knew it was foolhardy to ask this woman to drive on a dark icy night, through the empty town to midnight mass, so that I could fulfill my need to to add my voice to the singing of Silent Night at midnight on December 24[th,] we piled into Anna's old car to drive through the snowy, shut down, picture postcard town to church.

The car window was fogging up. "Oh, dear, oh," Anna mumbled," while fumbling with her gloved hand for the appropriate button on the dashboard. "The defroster didn't work."

Fogged window and all, we did arrive at the church. Anna found a spot to park her car in the crowded, well lit parking lot.

In the packed Episcopal Church, the pre-service carol singing was already in progress. We were greeted by a smiling young man, in a dark green suit. He wore a tie in a red and green flower print that briefly brought back a memory of a textile I had once designed in my past. Anna had been raised Russian Orthodox. During our foggy car ride she admitted that she had not been to any church for ever. I could feel her hesitancy following a step behind me and the young man showing us to good seats in a pew close to the altar. The usher handed us both programs.

In the seat in front of us a large lady dressed in a riotously vivid silk dress and black hat piled with flowers and veiling was seated next to a good old boy in blazer and plaid trousers. Both turned around and treated us with welcoming smiles and Christmas greetings. A man seated on my right, handed me a hymnal. I reached for another one on the shelf before us hand to Anna.

The procession of the celebrants in white and green festive vestments and the robed choir entered from the refectory and came down the center aisle. The elaborate cross was carried by a young woman with long blond tresses. She was flanked on each side by two attendants, followed by the pastor, the ministers, the acolytes. Then came the incense bearer swinging the filigreed brass vessel on a chain. The church was quickly filling with the sweetish odor of incense. I looked around at this assembly of worshippers perfectly tailored to the Christmas scene in a lilywhite small town in New England. Across the aisle, the frail old lady who could not stand without assistance from the dutiful family members at her side. The whitehaired gentlemen and their wives in tartan skirts and velvet blazers, with sensibly trimmed short haircuts. Pale young girls in red or green velvet dresses, with hair gathered into polite ponytails tied with ribbons. Throughout the church, there were couples, hushing small children, brought by their parents, perhaps to experience their first Christmas Mass who, before they were tucked into their beds to dream of the treasures of morning, that would be left for them by Santa under the Christmas tree.

  When the front of the processional passed our pew, I bowed along with the congregants. Billy's aunt did not bow. The very old lady with her body trapped in a permanent bow in the aisle across from us, did not have to. At her side a middle aged man, maybe a son or in-law, was steadying her. I genuflected, I participated in the responses. I sang. My voice blended with the fresh young voices and the shaky, croaking ones of the elderly and rose to the simple, graceful wooden arches above us. Once again I was the anonymous Christmas visitor at the table. None of these people would ever know of the Nazis charging into the chapel of the Benedictine convent, in Kraków on December 25th 1944, to round up what remained there of Jews hiding in plain sight. Among strangers on a dark night in a town in New England, I am a pretender who has tucked herself into the embrace of Christmas, to join in the recitation of the Credo and the Lord's Prayer. I knew my lines. No one would suspect me. I would pass.

In the part of the service when people extend the Greeting of Peace, the fairly recent Ecumenical addition to the Mass, Anna, the less experienced church goer was taken aback by the sudden outburst of, shaking hands, embracing strangers. I shook hands with the young man who had passed me the hymnal, the lady in the elaborate hat, the gentleman in plaid trousers in the pew in front of us.

"Peace be with you," I was basking in a glow of goodwill. "Peace be with you." I meant it. "Peace be with you," I hugged Anna. "Merry Christmas."

The minister who delivered the sermon was a slim, beautiful patrician woman of uncertain age. Her graying blond hair was cropped short and neat in a style I have come to associate with members of the Episcopal female clergy or aging British actresses. Her sermon, suitable to the season, was a childlike story, an "uplifting" story, about a little girl who lived with her parents who were part of an international medical corps in a war torn country.

The little girl had tried to gather, as best as she could, materials and figures to construct a crèche. She had been hesitant about the few little toys she possessed. Substituting a small teddy bear, an elephant, a plastic frog, for the sheep and cow and donkey she knew were the animals that ought to be surrounding the manger. A clown doll was going to be the Joseph.

"Do you think this is good, mama," she had asked with each selection. Her mother thought it was just fine. Especially the choice of a Barbie in a nurse's uniform with a red cross printed on the bodice that made a perfect Mary. Not having a toy for the baby, the little girl finally came up with the inspired choice of a lighted candle stump for the Christ child. The parents were enchanted with their daughter's imagination and her understanding of Christ as a shining light.

Well, yes, the minister went on to tell that there had been an attack on the village. The little girl and her family, hiding in an underground cellar, had survived the burning of the upper part of the house. Throughout the delivery of her sermon, a perfect glow of a toothy smile never left the face of the minister. Hers was a calculated performance. When her sermon was finished I had to stop an impulse to applaud. But I couldn't help thinking that, war torn land or not, the house fire might have been started by the candle stump Christ child.

We arrived at the singing of "Silent Night," the peeling of twelve strokes of the church bell and the final triumphal booming postludium from the organ accompanying the exiting participants in Christmas Eve Midnight Mass that had welcomed the Christ child once again into the world and to Hanover, New Hampshire. As is the custom, the people filing out of the church were greeted by the officiating minister and celebrants.

Before heading out into the icy night, before climbing back into Anna's old Toyota, I wanted to stay connected to these strangers for another few moments.

Barely stopping myself from saying, "good show" to the minister, I said;

"Thank you for that lovely sermon." Face to face she really looked not unlike Vanessa Redgrave. She visibly basked in the certainty that she had given a good performance.

As if presenting a passport, adding legitimacy to my participating in Christian Christmas, I prolonged my moment with the minister: .

"The story in your sermon reminded me of the book of contemporary nativity poems I just read to a little girl." I felt unctuous, but couldn't stop myself from tacking on the coda, saying:

"The pictures showed the manger surrounded by elephants and tigers.... it even included a rat!" I didn't tell her that I had illustrated the book.

The minister, her beatific smile never leaving her face, shook my hand.

"Oh, but then, we do know!.. " she said, "The Hindus are so very inclusive."

Huh? Hindus? Where did they pop up from? I was stunned. I had been misunderstood.

"Are they," I said to the syrupy woman. "Are the Hindus inclusive?"

What about the caste system, I thought.... Did she read my thought?

The smile on the face before me was dimming visibly.

Tossing a quick "Merry Christmas" behind me I hurried out after Anna.

"What did she say to you," Anna asked when we got in the car. "Why,..was it, I wonder, yes.."

She turned her attention to the defroster problem again. Anna wouldn't have dreamed of starting a chat with a total stranger, who might never again cross her path. Two minutes into the short night ride through the pretty, snowy deserted town, with Anna peering cautiously through her un-defrosted car window, it came to me. Of, course, the elephants and the tigers....

"Anna," I said. "She thought I was Indian, East Indian."

The self confident member of the new, inclusive Episcopal clergy, so bolstered by the glow of her own performance, had presumed the right to let her light shine upon all God's children! In that congregation filled with blond and grey haired New Englanders, there I had been, with my long dark hair, my brown eyes, auslander.

"You should have told her you were Jewish." Anna's moment of wit outsmarted me.

"Of course, I should have!" I laughed. I wish I had been quicker on the uptake. "How witty of you, Anna!"

At that moment I felt a great affection for Billy's aunt, and forgot about the defroster.

On Christmas morning, I added prunes that had been soaking overnight to the peeled and chopped apple and onion mixture. I spooned it into the very large, emptied of innards, goose cavity. I folded the skin over the stuffing and crisscrossed a fresh piece of string over the steel pins that I had remembered to buy at a household supply store before we left New York. It was all messy but lusty and promising.

"This is no way to work," Billy said, coming into the kitchen. "You have to have a clean surface. You have to have order."

He moved with the full force of a determined commandant sweeping the not very efficient kitchen counters of scraps of stuffing remnants. Just as the day before, he had crushed and removed all the mailing boxes that Anna had stacked by the door.

"Yes, Willie, yes." Anna always spiced with extra affection the playing on his name. She, who had no children of her own adored her nephew. I never knew Billy's mother, who had serious bouts of depression and died young of cancer after a miserable marriage to Billy's father. Anna had made a promise to her dying sister that she would be a mother to the young man.

By the time we began to pick out and open one by one the presents from under the Christmas plant, the apartment was pleasantly perfumed with the lingering smells from morning coffee and fresh pastries, now augmented with the aromas of the roasting goose.

The presents Anna and Billy and I were about to exchange were not weighted with holiday importance. Billy unwrapped a package with several small bottles of cleaning fluid for eyeglasses from Anna. Anna unwrapped our present to her, a Japanese teapot, two cups and saucers, and little packages of an assortment of teas. For me Anna had a small vase from a local glass blower. There were three cans of fancy French sardines to Billy from me. And three pairs of socks. Billy presented me with a cell phone, the smallest, neatest object imaginable.

My boyish, blond, one eyed, gorgeous Billy. Thinned hair now. Cleaning his glasses. Only one lens needs attention. The other eye gone forever with his antique biplane, the crumpled yellow butterfly, on that Vermont farmer's field behind his professor's house.

It was time to open the presents from my son and daughter-in-law and granddaughter from California that Anna had taken out of the mailing box and arranged under her plant festooned with a string of Christmas lights. I unwrapped a coffee table book about a shoe designer. An amusing tee shirt with studs forming a star. A small enameled tray portraying cats cavorting in an artist's studio, some classic films on DVD for Billy.

"How nice," I kept saying. "How thoughtful." I wasn't going to admit the presents I was opening were a somewhat perfunctory obligations. Billy knew very well the care and time and money I had spent on the gifts I had sent.

"Aren't you overdoing it?" he had rolled his eyes, when I was preparing the huge box for pick up by FedEx.

On the East coast daylight was beginning to fade. It was time to relight Anna's collection of thick candles.

The roasting goose needed to be looked at. Anna hovered while I opened the oven door and lifted the heavy pan placing it onto a towel on the counter Billy had cleaned so well. I removed the dome of tin foil. The big bird, cradled in the v-shaped rack was roasting according to schedule. A deep pool of grease had already collected in the bottom of the pan. The slowly measured cooking process was tempering the bird's dead muscles and sinews, loosening flesh from bone. The meaty thighs clinging close to the body were almost done, according to the cooking instructions, ready when "the juices run clear." The butcher had chopped off the useless lower legs at the knee joint. Not so long ago the bird had promenaded and honked and chased other geese on green grass. The two other protrusions, the remnants of powerful flapping wings, stiffly hugged the sizzling carcass. I replaced the tinfoil and slid the pan back onto the oven rack. Billy was sharpening a large not very promising knife.

When the bird was ready I transferred it with some trepidation from the roasting pan to a platter. I poured off the drippings to whip up a traditional gravy. I shook the parboiled potatoes in the butter and sugar glaze. The red cabbage was reheating on the stove.

Anna basked in the company of her darling nephew and his bustling lady. I knew she welcomed the different set of sounds and putterings. An interlude in her self-protective daily routine. I had not set out to have a thrilling time, but I really wasn't having a bad one.

It was when I called California on my new cellphone that my small, unexciting, very well planned Christmas with Billy's aunt Anna in New Hampshire, shattered.

"What charming presents," I cooed into my new cellular phone. "And the wrappings were so nice."

My voice, adjusted to the proper holiday melodiousness and motherly affection, poured into the compact three-inch box of communication at my ear and traveled on inexplicable waves from the east to the west coast. My daughter-in-law was busy in her kitchen. She sounded distracted. "I am cooking dinner for six grown-ups and four kids." No comments on my gifts.

I asked if my son's leather jacket fit. Oh, sure it was fine. I went down the list asking how he had liked his British cashmere sweater, how she had liked her silk shirt, the book on Matisse, how had the kid liked her party dress, etc. etc. Everything was perfect. I felt more and more foolish and deflated. I had expected more gushing. I had expected my son and granddaughter to pop into the conversation.

And then, through the tiny receiver clutched to my ear, from the coast on the other side of the land where it was twelve o'clock noon, came a question from my daughter-in-law.:

"How did you like your chain and pearl necklace?" What in the world was she talking about? What necklace?

"Haven't you opened it?" I listened, helpless, while my son's wife described a platinum chain inset with pearls she and my granddaughter had found in a hip jewelry boutique on Montana Avenue in Santa Monica.

"The little pink box," she said. With the purple ribbon and the flower sprig." No such gift had been among the presents I had opened. I panicked.

"You have to take another look," my daughter-in-law said. "We're here. Call back."

I sat there with Billy's Christmas gift silent in my hand. In my head the vision of Anna emptying the presents out of the California UPS box. And Billy crushing boxes and packing materials and carrying them out to the garbage.

"She must have missed the little box among the peanuts!" I said to Billy. "Your aunt had no business opening the mailing box from California."

"I told her she could," Billy looked sheepish.

"I.. what, no,.." I didn't.. no, I.. "Anna was completely flummoxed. "What peanuts?"

"You and your stupid cleaning," I hissed at Billy. "You threw out my present. Just tossed it." I was crushed. "Both of you did."

Anna kept mumbling, looking toward the sliding glass door. I started hating her for not knowing what packing peanuts were. Hating her hesitant, incomplete phrases, her fluttering, her surreptitious turning off of lights to save electricity! That was it. She sat in the dark. It was easy to miss one small box hiding in the packing materials when she took out the other presents and arranged them under the plant, the ersatz Christmas tree, in her unlit apartment until we walked in. And Billy's rules and tactics for cleaning and order. I hated him. I hated his aunt. I hated everything connected to him and her and the docile, uninformed, churchgoing people of New England. I wished I had gone to California. Or stayed in New York to have Christmas with my daughter and some of her theatre friends.

Billy was throwing on his parka and heading for the door. "I'll go through the garbage in the dumpster," he said calmly.

Anna was already putting on her big sweater, ready to follow him. I grabbed a throw from a chair and trooped through the snow in my flat, thin indoor shoes. I felt hopeless. Crushed. Betrayed. I said nothing. I didn't feel the cold. All I could think of was my pretty, charming granddaughter, her little hand reaching up to the store counter, fingering the necklace I would never see, proudly telling the salesclerk what a perfect Christmas gift she and mama had been so clever to find for her niania.

The tall dumpster in the center of the condominium circle, was filled to the brim with freshly discarded boxes and Christmas wrappings. It was neat suburban trash, as proper as the church people from the night before.

Billy climbed up onto the heap. Balancing, bending over, he was plunging his arms and hands into the crumpled recently discarded packing materials. Christmas day. Freezing cold on a dark late afternoon in New England.

"Here are some packing peanuts," Billy's voice came from where he was bent in half, disappearing into the overflowing mass of wrapping paper and crumpled cardboard boxes, big and small, sinking into crinkling garbage filling the dumpster.

"You know that this is futile." I sighed. I was spent, resigned.

How in the world could one possibly imagine that a tiny box would not be lost forever in this jumbled mess. I was shivering. I wanted to go home. To New York.

Billy's head reappeared over the edge of the dumpster. He rose to the surface balancing himself on the rim and stood tall on top of the heap of garbage. Grinning, hovering above us, his right arm lifted in the air, like that of the Statue of Liberty. In lieu of the lighted torch, his hand held a little unharmed box, wrapped in pink paper, tied with a pale green ribbon with a sprig of miniature dried flowers attached.

"It's a miracle," laughed my very Jewish daughter-in-law, when I called. "It's a real, fucking Christmas miracle." I heard happy noises and applause erupt in the California household. She was back on the phone: "Do you like it?"

I hadn't even removed the ribbon or paper from the little box when I rushed to make the call on my new phone!

"Whatever it is I will love it," I cried.

I sat on Anna's sofa, trembling, with the gift in my hand and forgiveness in my heart. When I finally opened the miraculously retrieved box, I found a very pretty medium length chain of platinum, somewhat resembling a bicycle chain. Inserted in each link was a small pearl. It was a chic necklace for a young, snappy person. Or for a hip older one. An object to flatter a woman who had loved for a time to ride on the back of a motorcycle and also loved to hang pearls around her neck when she went to the opera. Or sat on a barstool. It was a thoughtful, witty gift. I loved it.

We sat down to the goose dinner. In spite of the make-do knives in Anna's kitchen, Billy managed to carve the roasted bird into presentable thin slices. I had shaken the potatoes to their glazed perfection. The red cabbage, reheated, tasted as it should, better than the day before. The jar of Swedish lingon berries I had brought from New York City added the right touch to my properly prepared Swedish Christmas dinner.

Billy, relieved after the drama of the necklace in the dumpster, was eating lustily. "Goose meat tastes gamey," he said, reminding himself, his aunt, me, of his hunting days with his father. "Almost like a deer steak. I like it."

"Yes,... delicious,.. yes," Anna agreed. "A new experience for me,..yes.."

If the dark, somewhat stringy meat of the decimated bird didn't exactly repulse me, it didn't really tempt me either. The Christmas dinner was just something to end the day with. My hand kept reaching up to my neck. I was convinced that if I didn't keep touching it, my necklace would evaporate.

The pearl studded chain was a generous but obligatory Christmas gift. Over time it would become just another thing, a bauble to hang around my neck or keep in a jewelry box. But, right there and then, on the fading day of December, in a small apartment in a northern town on the East Coast of America, the value of the little bit of metal and nacre warming my neck could never be assessed by a jeweler.

The next morning the three of us embraced. Anna was thanked for her hospitality. Billy put our bags in the trunk of the rented car. Christmas with his aunt Anna in Hanover, New Hampshire was over.

"Let me drive, Billy Goat" I said. He gave me an indulgent smile and handed me the key.

The sun was shining. The hoarfrost was melting. The road was perfectly plowed. Behind the wheel in this blinding white winter landscape, I concentrated soberly on my driving. Billy, in the passenger seat, was checking out features on my new cell phone. Against my skin, under the sweater and coat and scarf, I could feel the necklace.

I remembered other rides with Billy in a variety of cars and weathers. With warnings of summer storms crackling on the radio in his new, used BMW on the road by the sea in Florida. In a rented car in France under gloomy gray skies in April on the way to the Normandy beaches. Careening in a jeep on the isle of Crete on the way to the palace of Knossos.

And, I thought of our first improbable, golden Vermont summer together. When, overwhelmed with love for the man at the wheel of his convertible I, with the wind whipping, wrapping hair around my face, not quite daring to trust these moments, feared that the ride, the man, our hurtling through the landscape would evaporate, just like that, at the next bend on the onrushing road.

We crossed the New Hampshire border under the "Welcome to Vermont" sign.

At the airport parking lot in Burlington we returned the rented car to Avis.

The Jet Blue plane was waiting, ready to take off for New York City.

Billy and I were going home.

Acknowledgments

I would like to thank several people who were instrumental in helping me with this book.

First, my writing professor at the New School, John Reed, whose quiet insightful observations inspired changes which always led to improvements in the manuscript.

Two colleagues in professor Reed's classes, Jhon Sanchez and Jimmy Biondolillo, who always encouraged me and laughed at me when I faltered.

A special thanks to my brother Bernhard and sister-in-law Mary, both doctors in psychology, for their sustaining and loving assurances when I caved into doubts.

My friend Flavia Destefanis, who read an early version of "StoneSoup" and corrected Italian phrases.

My friend Leslie Tetreault, who read an early version and encouraged me.

Aengus McGiffin, who urged me on after reading an early version.

Stephen O'Rourke, who, after reading an early version, encouraged me to continue.

And my son Adam, who patiently helped with screen sharing whenever the manuscript needed to be reformatted and sent out.

About the Author

Anita Lobel is well known for her colorful picture books. She is the creator of such classics as *Alison's Zinnia*, *Ducks on the Road* and *One Lighthouse, One Moon*. Her books have appeared on The New York Times best illustrated list, and her book *On Market Street* won a Caldecott Honor Medal.

Her childhood memoir *No Pretty Pictures: A Child of War* was a finalist for the National Book award.

Her books have been translated into many other languages, and continue to sell around the world.

Anita lives and works in New York City, her adopted home of long ago.

[298]

CPSIA information can be obtained
at www.ICGtesting.com
Printed in the USA
BVHW041245100323
660175BV00014B/1106/J